Leading for Excellence

A Twelve-Step Program to Student Achievement

Thomas Harvey,
Bonita M. Drolet, and
Douglas P. DeVore

ROWMAN & LITTLEFIELD EDUCATION

A division of
ROWMAN & LITTLEFIELD
Lanham • Boulder • New York • Toronto • Plymouth, UK

Published by Rowman & Littlefield Education
A division of Rowman & Littlefield
4501 Forbes Boulevard, Suite 200, Lanham, Maryland 20706
www.rowman.com

10 Thornbury Road, Plymouth PL6 7PP, United Kingdom

British Library Cataloguing in Publication Information Available

Library of Congress Cataloging-in-Publication Data
Harvey, Thomas, 1946–
  Leading for excellence : a twelve step program to student achievement / Thomas Harvey, Bonita M. Drolet and Douglas P. DeVore.
    pages cm
  Includes bibliographical references and index.
  ISBN 978-1-61048-982-9 (cloth : alk. paper) — ISBN 978-1-61048-983-6 (pbk. : alk. paper) — ISBN 978-1-61048-984-3 (electronic) 1. Motivation in education. 2. Academic achievement. 3. Educational leadership. I. Title.
  LB1065.H328 2014
  370.15'4—dc23
                                                                    2013045614

♾TM The paper used in this publication meets the minimum requirements of American National Standard for Information Sciences—Permanence of Paper for Printed Library Materials, ANSI/NISO Z39.48-1992.

Printed in the United States of America

Contents

Examples, Forms, and Charts

Preface

We guarantee it!

We guarantee that you will achieve a high-achieving school environment if you follow this 12-step program—all you have to do is follow the principles of:

Step One	Strong Leadership
Step Two	Culture of High Achievement
Step Three	Vision and Values
Step Four	High Expectations
Step Five	Love and Passion
Step Six	Focus on Learning
Step Seven	Embedded Professional Development
Step Eight	Assessment and Evaluation
Step Nine	The Strength of Teams
Step Ten	Collaboration and Shared Decision Making
Step Eleven	Communication
Step Twelve	Flexibility and Resilience

These are in essence stepping stones to achieving success, 12 steps to crafting a high-achieving environment. A number of steps you may be outstanding in; some you may be weak at. You may take larger strides than others if you're not already doing some of them. But these are the stepping stones to attaining a high-achieving environment.

But this is dependent on six assumptions:

Assumption 1

You've got to really want it! You need to have a passion for high achievement and be willing to do anything to reach a high-achieving environment. You cannot be halfhearted about following the principles included in this book. You'll make mistakes. But you must go on pursuing all efforts to achieve your goal. If you're seriously intent on achieving an environment that emphasizes success in all its forms—academic, arts, success, athletes, and the like—you'll be one step closer to achieving it. You've passed this premise.

Assumption 2

You need to be willing to get everyone on the bus! In order to reach your goal of high performance, you must have an operational, high-performing team you are working with. This may mean you need to develop some people, fire some people, promote some people, and encourage all people. It takes guts to do this. You have to make serious assessments of all your employees and then meddle in their professional lives. You have fierce conversations. It would be far easier and safer to ignore their skills and talents and let them be. Let the ship run on its own.

But you are a leader. You must give direction. You must build the strongest team possible to serve children's needs. You must, as Collins (2001) says, get everyone on the bus, but the right people on the bus.

Assumption 3

You have scant but adequate resources. This must seem like a strange assumption, at least the part about scant resources. The adequate is obvious—you must have the resources to do the job. Whether it may be in the form of budget money or people or facilities or time or even in energy, you've got to have the resources commensurate with the tasks required.

But scant is another thing. This assumption comes from research I did many years ago (Curtis and Harvey, 1976). I found that scant resources, but adequate, led to the highest degree of accomplishment. People would replace money with ingenuity, innovativeness, and good ideas. "Necessity is the mother of invention" is apt here. If you want a high-achieving environment, then you need adequate, not lush, resources.

Where resources were scant, you couldn't do things in the same old ways. People had to think up ways to get the job done. Invention took the place of resources and whenever invention takes place, the institution works for the better.

It is not too surprising in these tight times that institutions have scarce resources. But rather than bemoan the situation, take advantage of it. Be more ingenious. Be more innovative. Be more inventive. But keep on fighting for those scarce resources. You must have adequate ones.

Assumption 4

You have at least one year of experience. If you're in your first year as a principal or superintendent, you cannot produce a high-achieving environment. You must listen to all constituents. You must assess the people and environment. It takes experience with the people of the organization to institute the principles contained in this book.

On the other hand, you can't be a year away from retirement. You neither have the energy nor willpower to produce a high-achieving environment. Just pass on the recommendation to read our book to your successor.

That leaves most of you. You've got no excuses, unless . . .

Assumption 5

You are incompetent. Then it doesn't matter what you want to do. You are not capable leaders.

But we assume you are competent. You may be dispirited by the relentless attacks on education or you may be worn down by the multitude of tasks required of you. Or you may be saddened by lack of support your community gives you.

But remember, you are not incompetent. You are a leader. Leaders get up when pushed down; brush themselves off and do their best from this day forward.

But if you are incompetent, get out of the way, so real leaders can lead. Resign now.

If you're not incompetent, then get on with the business of leading your organization to high achievement.

Assumption 6

Last, but not least, you have got to have a sane board. The criteria for sanity:

- They operate as a team.
- They are agreeable, but not always in agreement.
- They have the best interest of the children in their minds and souls.
- They are attentive to the issues of education.
- They don't try to micromanage.
- They are mentally and physically competent.
- They don't have a personal agenda except what is good for schools.

Crazy boards do exist. They are damaging to schools and the purposes of education. If you have such a board, then board development is what you must do, if you have any hope of attaining a high-achieving environment.

You must make a crazy board sane. We will not take the time to posit solutions to a crazy board. There are a number of resources available to you through the National School Boards Association and others to solve this problem. We simply say solve it before it kills the district!

ORGANIZATION OF CHAPTERS

If you've satisfied all the assumptions contained in this chapter, you're ready to read the 12 steps to establishing a high-achieving environment.

Each chapter is organized into three parts. After an introductory paragraph, each chapter will:

1. Describe the principles that you should follow to accomplish each step
2. Posit some practical suggestions you could implement
3. List possible readings to help elucidate the issue; no extra reading is required though.

We will end the 12 steps with a complete listing of all the principles.

BREVITY

These principles are not very complex. They may be difficult to implement, but in their explanation, they are relatively simple to understand. As such, we can briefly explain them. We do not need to go on and on and on. They are obvious.

In addition to the brevity of the chapters, there are not a myriad of references. There are enough references to prove the case, but they are not a literature chapter in a dissertation. If you wish to follow up on the literature presented in these chapters, then you can consult the additional readings listed in each chapter.

Our intent is to write it, get out of the way and, then, let you get on with the hard work of leading your organization to a high-achieving environment.

VOICE

One last thing needs to be said about the voice we use. We will tell stories in the first person, either "I" or "we." This may mean "I, Bonnie," or "I, Tom" or "I, Doug." It doesn't matter to us, nor should it to the reader. Not all of the stories are our own. Some are the stories of colleagues that we have observed as they engaged in their own struggles with achieving success. What matters are the story and the point it serves.

Chapter One

Strong Leadership

If your actions inspire others to dream more, learn more, do more and become more, you are a leader.

—John Quincy Adams

The importance of the leadership role has been established in the literature as evidenced by the Wallace Foundation research that reports successful leadership plays an extremely significant role for improving student learning (Louis, Leithwood, Wahlstrom and Anderson, 2010). Their research also points out that the role of leadership is often underestimated regarding the impact on the ability of any district or school to raise their student achievement levels. The importance of the role of leadership is summed up as: "Leadership is important because it sets the conditions and the expectations in the school that there will be excellent instruction and there will be a culture of ongoing learning for the educators and for the students in the school" (Louis et al., 2010).

Jill Jacoby (2003), in an article for the Johns Hopkins University School of Education publication states: "The importance of leadership cannot be overstated in an environment where the goal is that every student will achieve at high levels." We believe understanding the importance leadership plays in student achievement is the first step toward reaching and sustaining higher student achievement.

The seven principles of leadership discussed in this chapter will establish the link to the importance of leadership and the overall connection to increasing student achievement. The next 11 chapters of the book's 12-Step approach will provide further evidence and support for how these seven leadership principles lead to high achievement for all students:

A STRONG LEADER ESTABLISHES A
CLEAR VISION FOR THE ORGANIZATION
THAT ALL STUDENTS CAN ACHIEVE

A vision for a district or school site can take different forms, but it is a statement about what the organization wants to become in the future based on their values and the relationship to their mission. The importance of establishing a clear vision that focuses on student achievement cannot be underestimated. As a former superintendent I have experienced time and again the difficulty of staying focused on the vision when I would find myself caught up with the everyday distractions and concerns that act to move your focus away from the vision. A clear understanding of where your organization needs to be directed is paramount.

Volumes have been written on the role of a leader in establishing a common vision and motivating all members of an organization to act upon that vision. John Kotter (1996, p. 25) states: "Leadership defines what the future should look like, aligns people with that vision, and inspires them to make it happen despite the obstacles." Peter M. Senge wrote the following in the *Fifth Discipline* (2006, p. 192).

> A shared vision is not an idea. It is not even an important idea such as freedom. It is, rather a force in people's hearts, a force of impressive power. It may be inspired by an idea, but once it goes further—if it is compelling enough to acquire the support of more than one person—then it is no longer an abstraction. It is palpable. People begin to see it as if it exists. Few, if any, forces in human affairs are as powerful as shared vision.

The research tells us that most people in an organization do watch and tend to follow the examples of their leaders. The role of the leader is key in sharing and promoting a vision that is "inspired," "compelling," and "palpable" within the organization for all students achieving at a high level. Chapter 3 on Vision and Values will provide greater insight into a leader's role and strategies for promoting a vision of what supports increased student achievement.

A STRONG LEADER DEVELOPS AND
ADHERES TO GOALS THAT FOCUS
ON STUDENT ACHIEVEMENT

Developing a strong vision, as previously discussed, is certainly a key step toward achieving greater student achievement. However, the vision is the big picture you have established for the future. Once a strong vision is established it becomes imperative that action-oriented goals be established to guide the organization toward the vision's future state and to provide benchmarks for progress along the journey to higher student achievement.

One example of the role of action-oriented goals comes to mind when I think about a "vision" my wife and I set in early spring. Our vision was to travel to Romania in fall and explore the beauty and history of the many castles and medieval towns. We had a clear vision of what we wanted in the future, but had we just relied on the inspiration of that vision we would have never made it a reality. Instead, we collaboratively set several action-oriented goals that would guide us to accomplishing the vision. I am happy to report the goals we set were strategically acted upon and we did happily experience our vision for travel in Romania.

This principle speaks to the importance of a leader's role in setting goals for student success. It has been said that a well-set goal is a goal that is already halfway reached. Like our recent trip to Romania, goals provide the road map for successfully reaching the intended destination. Sure, you may run across an occasional detour or an expected event that calls for some adjustment to the direction of a particular goal but you still remain directed toward the outcome, your vision for the future.

Successful leaders understand that the establishment of activity-based goals will provide direction for the entire organization toward the establishment of the vision for improved student achievement.

Strong leaders are constantly monitoring the progress of goals using benchmarks along the journey and making adjustments if needed to reach the vision-based, intended outcome. These leaders will seek the input of the staff, teachers, and administrators to determine the "how" to go about achieving those goals. They understand the importance of seeking input about the "how" and in doing so they are building a strong sense of shared ownership in the outcome of increased student achievement.

Chapter 10 on Collaboration and Shared Decision Making will speak directly to how leaders seek the input of staff to craft decisions that lead to accomplishing important goals. The chapter on Establish Clear Values, Tenets, and Goals will provide greater insight into a leader's role and strategies for establishing goals that lead to increased student achievement. This principle speaks to the importance of a leader's role in setting goals for student success.

A STRONG LEADER ENCOURAGES THE
GOOD IDEAS OF OTHERS

As stated in the previous principle and addressed in chapter 10 of this book, it is the seeking of good ideas from others about how to accomplish a goal that leads to the vision. A real strength of a successful leader is to seek and value the input of others as to how they can best accomplish the vision of higher student achievement.

Our federal government asked Kurt Lewin, founder of social psychology, to work with American housewives to change their buying, cooking, and eating habits during the 1940s. In his published research articles based on this work, he concluded that when people become involved in the problem and their ideas are valued in developing the actual solutions, they became very committed to the outcome compared to when people were given the solutions.

Leaders who encourage a climate that values the good ideas of others will not only develop actions that lead in increased student achievement, they will also generate a lasting commitment of the staff, teachers, and administrators to achieving the intended outcome (Darling-Hammond and McLaughlin, 1995).

Knowing that seeking good ideas of others is so important, we must pause to consider that in many districts, this climate of sharing does not exist. It has been stated that a leader really leads by example, whether they intend to or not. We have all experienced working with leaders that espouse seeking input when they state, "I am open to ideas or the opinions of others." Unfortunately, their behavior telegraphs a completely different message.

Have you ever been in a meeting or team situation when a sincere idea is proffered toward solving a problem and one of the first comments made by the leader is, "Oh, we tried that before and it did not work" or "I don't think that will work because . . . ." It is these types of comments from leaders that send a very negative message to others that their ideas are not valued. It may be that someone tried a version of the idea and failed, but it is the skilled leader who will allow others' ideas to percolate up, be encouraged, and discussed for the possibilities. These behaviors create a safe and creative environment that values the power of ideas of others.

It is not easy for strong leaders to take their goals for achieving the vision of greater student achievement to staff, teachers, and administrators and be comfortable with the fact that some may actually reject an idea or offer input on how to restructure key goals. Yes, it is difficult for a leader to face the uncertainty that comes with encouraging the input of others. It can open them to feeling rejected after all their hard work or it may lead to some conflict of thinking that will need to be managed. Yet the fear of rejection or managing a conflict of ideas is what must be overcome.

Some of the best ideas are born out of meaningful conversations that start with the sound of rejection or air of conflict. It is critical that leaders stay consciously aware that they do not have ownership of all the best ideas and perhaps not even the really good ones!

Leaders who have successfully increased the level of student achievement over time will often give credit to the ideas and actions of others beside themselves. Andrew Carnegie captured the essence of a great leader when he stated, "No person will make a great leader who wants to do it all himself, or to get all the credit for doing it" (Winston Churchill Leadership, para. 12 in Carnegie, 2012).

Great leaders do understand that they do not own all the good ideas and they can achieve very little without the commitment and support of the people who make up their organization. Chapter 10 on Collaboration and Shared Decision Making and Chapter 11 on Communication will provide more information on how to actualize the important principle of encouraging the good ideas of others.

A STRONG LEADER DOES THE RIGHT THING VERSUS DOING THINGS RIGHT

The lexicon of efficiency and effectiveness can lead one to believe they are very similar in meaning. During the early 1900s, in organizational studies by Taylor and Gilbreth the terms were used to describe time and motion studies that focused on getting the task done. However, by the 1980s the concept of efficiency and effectiveness took on a very different implication when the discussion focused on getting the task done but also on consideration for creating value and appreciation of people involved with that task.

Covey (1994) credits Peter Drucker with coining the phrase "management is doing things right; leadership is doing the right things," based on his understanding of scholarly leadership research that focused on the concepts of efficiency and effectiveness.

Strong leaders understand that there is more than one way to accomplish important work and achieve bold goals, such as higher student achievement for all students. These strong leaders focus on process and people to seek doing the right thing or creating alternative solutions for increasing student achievement.

There are frameworks a leader can employ to help them focus themselves and others on the need of shifting resources. One example is Daggett's (2012) International Center for Leadership in Education Four Quadrants Effectiveness and Efficiency Framework, designed to help discover innovative and successful practices and how to operationalize them in the face of declining resources.

The late Stephen Covey (2004) contrasted the difference between efficiency and effectiveness as, "Management is a bottom line focus: How can I best accomplish certain things? Leadership deals with the top line: what are the things I want to accomplish? . . . Efficient management without effective leadership is, as one individual has phrased it, like straightening deck chairs on the Titanic" (pp.101–102). Interesting that attempts to bring about change in K–12 education are sometimes referred to using the same phrase about "straightening deck chairs on the Titanic."

It can be difficult to lead by doing the right thing. Tony Blair (Daily Mail Online.com on Sunday, 1994) said "the art of leadership is saying no, not yes. It is very easy to say yes." To lead by doing the right thing means doing what is right or best for students and student achievement. This can sometimes fly in the face of conventional wisdom. There are times when making the decision to do the right thing involves more resources such as money or time.

Therefore, making the best decision to ensure a positive impact on student achievement may require the reallocation of resources such as money and time. Saying no to some for the sake of higher student achievement is not easy and can often lead to conflict with different groups competing for the scarce resources for a pet project of a board member or at the bargaining table.

The strong leader will have the courage to say no when it is necessary. They will seek out decision-making processes and ideas of others to help them discover the best action to take for increasing student achievement. Chapter 6, Focus on Learning and Academic Rigor, will provide more information on how to actualize the important principle of encouraging the good ideas of others.

A STRONG LEADER USES COLLABORATION

The relationship between strong collaboration and student achievement has also been well established in the literature. In fact, the push for developing a culture of collaboration in our schools has emerged from the scholarly research on schools that have proven themselves to be successful in significantly increasing student performance.

McLaughlin and Talbert (1993) conducted a longitudinal study that provided evidence that high schools and departments that foster a collaborative learning community environment were more effective in increasing student achievement. The Annenberg Institute for School Reform (Barnes, 2004) published a report on school improvement that found "opportunities for adults across a school system to learn and think together about how to improve their practice in ways that lead to improved student achievement" (p. 2). Goddard, Goddard, and Tschannen-Moran (2007) completed a study using 452 teachers in 57 elementary districts that established a statistical relation between teacher collaboration and student achievement using reading and math scores.

The relationship of a strong leader as the driver of establishing professional communities with a culture of collaboration has also been evidenced in research for many years. So if collaboration leads to higher student achievement and strong leaders are the drivers of establishing a collaborative environment, why are so many districts struggling to raise student achievement? Equally important, why are many schools and districts proclaiming to be learning communities focused on collaboration but not showing significant student achievement gains when compared to traditional schools?

Rick DuFour proclaims, "Leaders determined to impact student achievement must not settle for congeniality, coordination, delegating responsibilities, or any form of collaboration lite. They must promote a collaborative culture by defining collaboration in narrow terms: the systematic process in which we work together to analyze and impact professional practice in order to improve our individual and collective results" (2003, p. 64). In other words, the strong leader needs to "do the right thing" when it comes to establishing collaborative environments that will result in higher student achievement.

In the age of No Child Left Behind, legislation tends to focus more on the "what" about knowledge and less about the "how." It is not hard to understand why leaders may be giving lip service to "collaboration lite" rather than committing the resources to provide the time and structure to establish a collaborative culture that results in greater student achievement. Often the conventional thinking believes if we restructure the schedule to give teachers time to work together, good things will happen. In reality, time for teachers to collaborate is just the first step. The strong leader understands that establishment of the structure for collaboration is a key factor.

Training teachers as leaders to facilitate collaboration time, establishing norms and expectations for cooperation, is paramount to strong teams. It provides them with a framework to guide them toward looking at "what are we doing that works for increasing student achievement?" These are the beginning steps to support successful teacher collaboration. Chapters 6, 9, and 11 will provide more information on how to actualize the important principle of strong leaders using collaboration to improve student achievement.

A STRONG LEADER MANAGES THE RELATIONSHIPS OF THE INSTITUTION

One difference between being a manager or being a leader is that managers have subordinates; leaders have followers. There is an old saying that tells us that every leader needs to look back once in awhile to make sure he has followers. The whole theory area of leadership and followership is one that has received a lot of attention in the literature over the past couple of decades.

It is clear from this literature that people in an organization follow a leader because of that leader's transformational style and attention to the "soft skills" such as integrity, transparency, fairness, and even a sense of humor. Strong leaders of change develop these "soft skills" so they can lead by influencing people to willingly work toward an established vision and collaboratively developed goals.

Bennis (2003) has described leaders as those who can guide people to feel they are worthy and can achieve the vision and goals of the organization. This is not an innate ability that has been given to the chosen few. The literature on leadership is prolific about the leadership traits that one can study and acquire to be a transformational leader for change.

There is also a depth of information about what successful leaders need in order to develop compelling vision, set goals with input from others, build relationships, influence others, and get things done. *Strengths Based Leadership* by Rath and Conchie was published in 2008 using a comprehensive analysis of the Gallup landmark 30-year StrengthsFinder assessment study. After analyzing more than 1 million surveys and over 10,000 interview transcripts of followers about what influential leaders do to enhance their lives and motivate them to follow, they found the four basic needs were trust, compassion, stability, and hope (Rath and Conchie, 2008).

The strong educational leader, who desires to have followers embrace, believe in, and act on the vision of high student achievement for all students, needs to manage the relationships of the institution by focusing on trust, compassion, stability, and hope. Trust is earned and establishes a foundation for success. A strong leader is always conscious of their actions matching their words for they understand that trust takes time to gain, but can be lost quickly and is very hard to regain.

I recall a number of years ago a union grievance chair was meeting with me about a very delicate situation. We had proposed a solution that was not exactly what they wanted to hear, but it was directed at what was best for all, not just a single person. The grievance chair accepted the resolution by saying "we will trust that this is a sincere resolution and you will work to make it happen because so far you have not written a check we could not cash."

Trust is about what the leader does, not so much about what the leader says. It speaks to consistency and predictability over time. Leaders can promote trust by focusing on being transparent, sharing important information, and giving voice to concerned parties when decisions are being made.

Developing compassion or a caring environment can be a delicate balance for leaders. Some leaders actually avoid developing close relationships with others in the organization because they fear the problems that can arise from being perceived as too friendly or not sincere, and are concerned about what will happen if you have to make a decision that is not popular with that person or group of people.

These are real issues that a leader should consider when managing the level of compassion in their organization. But there is a much greater downside to not establishing a compassionate, caring environment that fosters friendships and allows followers to feel like their leaders do care about them.

Rath and Conchie's (2008) findings indicate that this is a huge issue in most organizations and must be managed, as evidenced by their statement, "We've seen that if people don't have close friendships on the job and if they don't have a supervisor or leader who really cares about them individually, there's almost no chance that they'll be engaged in their work" (Rath and Conchie, 2008).

The management of stability in the life of the organization is an important role for successful leaders. We live and work in very volatile, unstable times. Staff, teachers, and administrators are seeking stability in their work place and are often facing instability that stems from very difficult challenges and a feeling that there is no direction for a successful or positive outcome.

This is especially true as disagreement and conflict arise over the demands of No Child Left Behind, the new Common Core Standards, and the ever-changing, volatile political landscape. Conflicts will always be a part of a viable, living organization. It is not having conflict that makes for a stable organization; it is not addressing and managing conflict that exacerbates instability and causes toxicity that leads to lack of productivity.

Providing leadership by establishing a strong vision, collaborative goals, and norms for behavior; developing a climate of trust; and developing positive relationships will go a long way in producing a more stable climate for your employees to work and thrive.

Last is the role of leadership in establishing hope in the organization and followers. This is last because it involves the first three. You cannot establish a sense of hope in others without developing trust. If the followers in your district are feeling unsure in an atmosphere of instability, they cannot effectively work toward a future that will truly produce greater student achievement.

The positive climate that exists from leading with compassion and building meaningful relationships feeds the individual's and the organization's collective sense of hope regarding their vision to meet the needs of children and increase student achievement. Chapters 2, 3, and 5 will provide more information on how to actualize the important principle of strong leaders' managing the relations of the organization.

Therefore, the following six principles lead to strong leadership:

- A strong leader establishes a clear vision for the organization that all students can achieve.
- A strong leader develops and adheres to goals that focus on student achievement.
- A strong leader encourages the good ideas of others.
- A strong leader does the right thing versus doing things right.
- A strong leader uses collaboration.
- A strong leader manages the relationships of the institution.

PRACTICAL SUGGESTIONS

These are some practical suggestions to implement strong leadership:

1. Develop a brief and simple vision statement you can communicate over and over in all settings. Ask yourself each day, "Did I communicate our vision for improved student achievement today?"
2. Establish a small network of other K–12 leaders focused on improving student achievement and meet with them at least once a month to discuss new strategies and what is working/what is not working.
3. Keep current on researched-based literature regarding the role of leadership in student achievement. Read a minimum of one article per week and/or one book per month. We recommend you start with *Investigating the Links to Improved Student Learning: Final Report of Research Findings* (Louis, K. S., Leithwood, K. , Wahlstrom, K. L., and Anderson, S. E., 2010).
4. Establish a Student Achievement Council to include key administrators, teachers, and parents. This council should meet regularly during the year to discuss the goal of improving student achievement. Provide members with guiding articles or books to generate discussion. Also invite local (county) and state experts in student achievement to speak when possible.
5. Become an active listener to the ideas of others. As Covey promotes, seek to understand before dismissing or taking action.
6. Encourage and model collaboration at all levels of your organization. Encourage a climate that supports teachers working collaboratively, establishes focused discussions during collaboration time, and provides professional development for building collaborative skills for teachers.

SOME BOOKS, ARTICLES, AND WEBSITES TO
SUPPORT STRONG LEADERSHIP

Barnes, F. D. *Making school improvement part of daily practice.* Annenberg Institute for School Reform at Brown University. 2004. Retrieved on August 12, 2012 from Annenberg Institute website: http://annenberginstitute.org/tools/guide/SIGuide_intro.pdf.

Bennis, W. G. *On becoming a leader.* Cambridge, MA: Perseus Publication. 2003.

Blair, Tony. Daily Mail Online.com on Sunday, 1994.

Carnegie, Andrew. BrainyQuote.com. Retrieved December 31, 2012 from BrainyQuote.com website: http://www.brainyquote.com/citation/quotes/quotes/a/andrewcarn130735.htm#6v0iswkkUCBcOgzt.00.

Covey, S. R. *The seven habits of highly effective people: Powerful lessons in personal change.* New York: Simon and Schuster. 2004.

Daggett, W. R. *Effectiveness and efficiency framework—A guide to focusing resources to increase student performance.* Retrieved on August 29, 2012 from International Center for Leadership in Education website: http://www.leadered.com/pdf/EE%20%20White%20Paper%20website%203.25.09.pdf.

Darling-Hammond, L., and M. W. McLaughlin. "Policies that support professional development in an era of reform." *Phi Delta Kappan,* 1995: 76(8), 597–604.

DuFour, R. "Leading edge: 'Collaboration lite' puts student achievement on a starvation diet." *Journal of Staff Development.* 2003: 24(3), 63–64.

Goddard, Goddard, and Tschannen-Moran. "A theoretical and empirical investigation of teacher collaboration for school improvement and student achievement in public elementary schools." *Teachers College Record.* 2007: 109(4), 877–896.

Jacoby, J. "The role of educational leadership in ensuring academic success for every child." *New Horizons for Learning.* 2003. Retrieved from the Johns Hopkins University website: http://education.jhu.edu/PD/newhorizons/Transforming%20Education/Leadership%20in%20Education/The%20Role%20of%20Educational%20Leadership%20in%20Ensuring%20Academic%20Success%20for%20Every%20Child/index.html.

Kotter, J. P. *Leading change.* Boston, MA: Harvard Business School Press. 1996.

Kouzes, J. and Barry Posner. *The leadership challenge* (4th ed.). San Francisco: Jossey- Bass. 2007.

Louis, K. S., K. Leithwood, K. L. Wahlstrom, and S. E. Anderson. *Investigating the Links to Improved Student Learning: Final Report of Research Findings.* The Wallace Foundation. 2010. Retrieved from the Wallace Foundation website: http://www.wallacefoundation.org/knowledge-center/school-leadership/key-research/Pages/Investigating-the-Links-to-Improved-Student-Learning.aspx.

McLaughlin, M. W., and J. E. Talbert. "Contexts that matter for teaching and learning." Stanford, CA: Center for Research on the Context of Secondary School Teaching, Stanford University. 1993.

Rath, T., and B. Conchie. *Strengths based leadership: Great leaders, teams, and why people follow.* New York: Gallup Press. 2008.

Senge, P. M. *The fifth discipline: The art and practice of the learning organization* (rev. ed.). New York: Doubleday. 2006.

Chapter Two

Establish a Culture
of High Achievement

Walk into any truly excellent school and you can feel it almost immediately—a calm, orderly atmosphere that hums with an exciting, vibrant
sense of purposefulness. This is a positive school culture, the kind that
improves educational outcomes.

—Craig Jerald

Most people entering a school in America can tell if it is a positive experience. Oftentimes, they can't tell you why they have those feelings, but they
do! It is merely the culture of the school they are inundated with. The culture
exists in how they are welcomed, how the students are behaving, the tem-
perament of the staff they interact with, what values are apparent, and most
importantly today—whether it is a culture of high achievement!

This culture determines whether students are actively engaged in learning, whether staff members enjoy their jobs, and whether there is a spirit of
active communication. Not all schools have a culture for high achievement;
some just need a little help toward becoming a positive culture and others are
downright toxic (Drolet and Turner, 2010).

To have a culture of high expectations and achievement a leader must em-
body the following principles:

IF IT'S TOXIC—TURN IT AROUND

There are researched steps for turning a toxic school around. The problem is
that most leaders just don't use them. In fourteen easy actions—well maybe
not so easy—a 21st-century leader can turn around an organization and

13

produce a positive culture where people want to be there and be productive (Drolet and Turner, 2010)!

I once worked with a school where the teachers agreed wholeheartedly that children DID NOT come first at their school! The teachers said they had families and private lives and those things came first. Teaching was just a job. They were bitter and transferred this attitude to their low socioeconomic students. No one really wanted to be at that school except the principal and she was bound and determined to turn things around!

We worked together for two years going through the steps below. The teachers slowly came onboard and the school began turning around. I knew it was all a success when late in the third year, when I was no longer working with the school, I stopped by for a surprise visit. The principal could hardly talk fast enough, telling me all of the changes that had occurred. Finally, she said, "Don't listen to me; let's go talk to some teachers."

We did and what I heard was amazing. They were energized, engaged, joyful, and putting children first at the school—and it showed. It was hard work, they all agreed, but it was definitely worth it!

The scenario of Lemming School that will be mentioned later in the chapter points to a similar toxic environment. Everyone was definitely doing their own thing and still not very happy! Whereas, the people at Joyful, you will see, arrive, well, joyful! They are ready to face the day with smiles and suggestions.

The list of the fourteen "easy" actions that are all research based are (Drolet and Turner, 2010):

1. Analyze the situation.
2. Develop core tenets/values.
3. Determine the shared vision for the future.
4. Develop norms for behavior.
5. Promote shared leadership.
6. Analyze the data.
7. Write clear goals and expected outcomes derived from the data.
8. Set high expectations.
9. Develop a communication system.
10. Incorporate a shared decision-making process.
11. Encourage shared tasks.
12. Provide for a safe environment.
13. Plan celebrations/recognitions—large and small.
14. Encourage storytelling.

You will need to implement them NOW with a toxic organization. The change you see will make the effort worth it! You can't produce a high-achieving environment if it's toxic. It's not enough to have a positive culture, but the opposite is true—there is not a high-achieving environment where toxicity exists.

ESTABLISH TRUST—BE OPEN AND HONEST

Trust does not just happen. As a school leader, establishing trust should be priority #1! Nothing of significance will happen without it. Wagner and Masden-Copas at the Center for Improving School Culture developed the School Culture Audit (2002) with one of the major foci being trust. Why? When you want to buy a car, do you stop and think about which cars people trust the most to be reliable? Which dealer is trustworthy—giving me the straight answers and not running me around in circles? Who is it I can trust with such a large purchase? You don't just go to the closest dealer. You want someone who will be open and honest with you!

So, too, do the teachers and staff around you stop and ask questions. Is my leader trustworthy? Is my leader open and honest? If the answers are yes, then your organization can move at high speed. If the answer is no, well, you have a lot of work to do. Nothing really happens without trust. You build trust in five ways (Harvey and Drolet, 2006):

- *Interdependence* is when I need you and you need me.
- *Consistency* happens when you are true from word to deed and from deed to deed.
- *Honesty* builds trust because honesty is based on integrity and everyone sees it.
- *Affability* supports trusting relationships because likable people are easier to trust.
- *Extension of Trust* means that those who give trust get trust—even if it is sometimes violated!

So, just as when buying a car, your staff will go to someone they trust. Make sure it is you!

MAKE PEOPLE WANT TO BE THERE

Let's look at that scenario of toxic Lemming School mentioned above to understand the importance of what the research says about promoting a positive culture before you can promote a high degree of student achievement. If they don't want to be there, you're not going to get very far.

At Lemming School another day dawns and teachers drag into school for the start of the day. Grumbling about "students who don't care" can be heard in the staff lounge. The principal arrives fuming because new guidelines about following through on assigned duties had just been given to the teachers the day before and they were already being ignored!

In the staff lounge the teacher assigned to parking lot duty was talking to her colleagues about the stupid rules the principal had sent out. "Do we look like children? We know when we have duty! No one is going to treat me like a child and get away with it. I just didn't show up for duty today!"

The principal notices quite a few stragglers walking the halls, both teachers and students. With a sigh, the principal approaches them to find out why they aren't in class. Many reasons are given, but none seem to have credibility.

Students in classrooms around the school do not have homework completed, teachers are upset, and the phones to the office begin ringing for the principal to "do something" with this student!

Teachers do not collaborate, working in isolation and come together only to complain about their work.

At the staff meeting, teachers arrive late and unfocused. The agenda is full of more things to do, decisions that have been made for the staff. No one wants to be there. No one wants to listen. And no one wants one more thing to do. And everyone wants to go home. Enough already! (Drolet, 2010)

If any part of this scenario is present in a school, the school is toxic. There is a lack of caring, a lack of trust, a lack of follow-through, a lack of learning, and a lack of respect. No one wants to work at this school and students definitely don't want to be there. The toxic culture is pervasive. If only it weren't so.

In the scenario above, the staff members drag into work each day. It may even be the principal or the superintendent! As the leader, it is important to turn that toxic environment around and make it a place where everyone—adults and children alike—want to be there. It's more than a leader's job, it's a duty!

Let's look at a corollary to the above scenario, Joyful School. Positive school culture has many definitions, but similar characteristics. You know when you see a positive culture and you lament when you don't. Phillips in 1996 stated that school culture is the shared experiences both in school and out of school (traditions and celebrations) that create a sense of community, family, and team membership.

The staff at Joyful High School arrives early to prepare for the day. Some have volunteered for before school activities, others are chatting in an upbeat way with colleagues and the principal is wending through all the activity with a huge smile and a "good morning" to everyone.

The first bell rings announcing the arrival of the students and teachers and staff take their places outside to greet students and start the day. Students yell hello and "high five" each other. Some stop and ask a teacher for some assistance. The day is off to a great start!

The classrooms are noisy with discussions and debates that are teacher monitored, but student directed. The principal finds that students can easily explain their learning.

After school, students leave with well thought out assignments and teachers begin to prepare for their professional learning communities.

This school is humming. What a difference!

Which school would you like to work at? Which school would you send your children to? Which school will have higher achieving students? I think you know the answer.

HAVE NORMS AND USE THEM

Anyone who has had a teenager knows that unless rules or norms are clearly stated, they will be abused, broken, and forgotten. "Come in by 11 p.m.? Oh, I thought you meant it was okay to be in by 11:30." We've all heard something like this. Schools need clear, precise, and shared norms that every adult needs to honor. Norms that are broken need to be recognized and discussed. Unfortunately, it is hard to confront a colleague, but people who work at successful schools do just that!

At one school we worked at, there was a norm for being on time, but one teacher—an excellent teacher, by the way—always broke the norm! She was late for everything! One day it was her turn to make a morning presentation at the staff meeting. The teachers all got together and decided not to show up at the 7:30 start time. They waited in their rooms until 7:40! The teacher and the principal were both wondering what was going on. Finally the teachers sauntered in. One spoke up and said, well, since Nora (the presenter) was always late, why should they be on time for her presentation! Nora was never late to another meeting! They all had a good laugh and reinforced the norm for being on time!

The best time to deal with broken norms is before they happen. It's up to the leader to make sure the norms are collectively developed and collectively reviewed. It only takes five to ten minutes at a staff meeting to review the norms and ask which ones aren't working so well. Ask questions as to why. What can we do differently as a team to make sure the norms are not ignored or broken? Having these discussions in advance, similar to discussing curfew with a teenager, will relieve a lot of stress and make for a much happier team.

USE ARTIFACTS, HEROES, AND STORIES

There is nothing like a great picture, good story, or a powerful hero to capture our imaginations and interest. Every organization has artifacts, stories and heroes.

Culture can be infused throughout the organization by expressing it in the artifacts of the organization. There are three types of artifacts in which an organization's culture can be expressed:

- *Physical artifacts* are physical objects and environments in the organization (e.g., pieces of artwork, furniture, rooms, meeting places, equipment).
- *Information artifacts* are primarily informational or computational (e.g., lists, directories, databases, computer applications).
- *Conceptual artifacts* are objects that we use in our mental or conceptual space (e.g., metaphors, stories, patterns, and so forth) (Culture in the Artifacts, May 2001).

So, when you think of your organization and the artifacts that people see, what do you think? At Zappos, the online shoe store, artifacts are all over the corporate offices and warehouses. They're there to express the "fun and weirdness" that management wants to instill in all of the workers. Their website has a great video of some of the artifacts that workers have developed to enhance the vision of fun and team that is Zappos (http://about.zappos.com/our-unique-culture/zappos-core-values)!

In your organization, is the artwork current and expressive of the organization's culture? Is it a Zappos fun place? Or is the artwork tattered and practically hanging off the wall? Does the staff lounge look like an afterthought or a cozy place where the staff really want to congregate and get to know one another? And does anybody tell a great story? Can you do a better job at getting your artifacts in order? Can they tell a really great story about your organization? I bet with a little help from your friends—now that people want to be there—you can really make your physical space a great space! Spend some time, and while you are at it, tell stories about the people who put up the artifacts you are taking down!

"Remember when. . . " stories highlight some of the greatest heroes and actions of the organization. In a school with a positive culture, Kent Peterson says, "There's an informal network of heroes and heroines" (1999). Whatever stories you tell, you must emphasize success. High achievement comes from the artifacts you display and the stories you tell!

KNOW YOUR STAFF MEMBERS' STORIES AND HONOR THEM

What do you know about each and every one of your staff members? Can you carry on a conversation about their personal lives? Do you know what their hobbies are? Do they know anything about you? It's time to get busy and start asking questions. Your current staff is full of stories and wonderful heroes and heroines. Spending time at staff meetings to talk about successes, off duty hobbies, and families will bring out lots of stories and more than a few hero and heroines.

I remember a staff member who was really having difficulty. When I sat down and began the courageous conversation with her, I found out that she donated incredible amounts of time to children's theatre and was an accomplished musician. She had never offered up those skills to me or to any other principal she had worked for. The more we talked the more excited she got about her "off duty" hobby. I asked her how she could make it happen at our school given money and time restraints. She went home, figured it out and went on to develop an incredible music and theatre program.

She became a hero and her story was well known not only around our school, but around the district. Sitting down and having conversations, whether courageous or social, are important and integral to success and high achievement.

CELEBRATE

You are going to hear this frequently. Celebrate, celebrate, celebrate. People want to jump on a band wagon, not on a hearse. They want to know they are appreciated. They want to know that what they do counts. Leaders who achieve success celebrate the small wins as well as the big ones, and they do it often.

Rick DuFour (1998) says "celebration is a fun and meaningful way to recognize accomplishments and reinforce shared values." And remember Zappos "Create Fun and A Little Weirdness."

One principal we worked with celebrated small improvements at her school by having a TGIF at her house. A superintendent handed out beautiful, fresh, red apples when it was time to celebrate someone's accomplishment. Celebrations can be an announcement over the loud speaker during student news broadcasts or they can be award certificates presented at a staff meeting for a job well done.

Take time to think about how many times you have celebrated improvements this year. Have you been chintzy in your celebrations or generous in recognizing results? The more generous you are, the more positive results you will have! The more you celebrate high achievement of all sorts, the more you get a high-achieving environment.

USE JOY—OFTEN!

The message you send is the message you receive! If you are not a joyful leader, you will not have a joyful staff. They will reflect your attitude. Let's return to Lemming School for a minute. Would you want to work there? The answer would be of course, "No way!"

I was working at a middle school once, much like Lemming, and I asked the simple question: "Would you send your child to this school?" I received a resounding "No" from the staff. It was dreary to be there.

Luckily, I was able to return throughout the year and as we developed their tenets and vision, they realized that they had been working in a fairly joyless environment. They made a commitment to turn that around and to be different. They wanted to be able to bring their own children to the school! They wanted to jump up each morning and be glad they were coming to this school! The leader took it all to heart and realized that the message she had been sending was not one of joy and that was exactly what had been received. She took responsibility and became the change she wanted to see!

It's time to remember that old Brownie song, "I've got something in my pocket, it belongs across my face. I keep it very close at hand, in a most convenient place. I'm sure you couldn't guess it if you guessed a long, long while. So I'll take it out and put it on, it's a Great Big Brownie Smile!" Show the joy whether you feel it or not. There are many days that leaders don't feel the joy. There are troubles at home, a suspension at school, a disciplinary action to take, but you just have to fake it! Joy begets more joy and joy begets energy to do the work to achieve success!

A FINAL NOTE

When we went on safari in South Africa, we experienced the most amazing example of the expectation of high achievement. As we rumbled along in our jeep during the very early hours, we came upon two elephants, literally tearing apart the forest.

Our guide shared that they were two teenage males that had been kicked out of the herd for bad behavior. The herd—especially the matriarchal head—would not allow such behavior to exist within her environment.

Elephants, we were told, are very bright and expect everyone to behave appropriately at all times. They had norms and a positive culture and anyone caught breaking those norms or infringing on the culture was kicked out until they could behave. Hence, our two male elephants were left alone in the forest to fend for themselves until they decided that the group culture of high achievement was more important to them than roaming aimlessly together and lonely.

This elephant syndrome should be a moral for all of us who are trying to engage everyone in high achievement. Sometimes, people need to be reminded that they aren't abiding by the culture that produces high achievement. Sometimes, they may need to be kicked out or asked to move on. We need to be strong. If an elephant can turn around a toxic environment, can't you?

Therefore, the following eight principles establish a culture of high achievement:

1. If it's toxic, turn it around.
2. Establish trust; be open and honest.
3. Make people want to be there!
4. Have norms and use them.
5. Use artifacts, heroes, and stories.
6. Know your staff members' stories and honor them.
7. Celebrate.
8. Use joy—often!

PRACTICAL SUGGESTIONS

These are some practical suggestions to establish a culture of high achievement.

1. Manage by walking around.
   You hear about it all the time, but do you do it? Calendar your walks so you don't let something else get in the way. Ask lots of questions and take lots of notes—and then follow through on any issues or concerns.
2. Analyze the situation at your school.
   Use the plethora of resources you will find in the References that can be implemented for analysis.
3. Identify the barriers to change by asking questions of everyone.
   Who isn't onboard? What's stopping your progress toward high achievement?
4. Develop core tenets/values.
   a. Bring your staff/parents together.
   b. Dialogue about what is important.

    c. Write six to eight tenet/value statements that will represent the core beliefs of the school.

    d. Incorporate them in written and oral communication.

5. Determine the shared vision for the future.

    a. Use the same or different group from above.

    b. With the core beliefs as a springboard, develop a shared vision of where the school should be in five years.

    c. Use metaphors and descriptive language to bring everyone along.

    d. Include the vision when talking about the future.

    e. Select artifacts, mottos, songs, and mascots that communicate the vision.

6. Develop norms for behavior

    Yes, yes, yes! Do it. I know we are all adults and should know how to act, but the reality is that it is research based that norms will help you build a positive culture to raise student achievement. You need to have the staff determine how everyone will behave and then hold people accountable for violating the norms.

7. Promote shared leadership

    a. Discover the strengths of every member of the staff.

    b. Use those strengths to encourage leadership behavior from everyone.

8. Analyze the data.

    a. Academic

    b. Attendance

    c. Use the data in developing goals and outcomes.

9. Write clear goals and expected outcomes derived from the data.

    a. Develop teams of teachers and staff members to work on various goals.

    b. Present them to the staff for input.

    c. Determine timelines.

    d. Write simple and doable action plans.

    e. Develop a curricular focus that is the responsibility of all.

10. Set high expectations.

    a. Make them clear to the students.

    b. Accept no excuses.

    c. Be consistent.

11. Develop a communication system.

    a. Build relationships through communication.

    b. Make sure everyone is on a need-to-know basis. Don't leave people out of the loop.

    c. Schedule collaboration time.

    d. Set expectations for communication and collaboration.

12. Incorporate a shared decision making process (Harvey, Bearley, and Corkrum, 1997).
    a. Include everyone or a leadership team as needed.
    b. Include problem finding.
    c. Include problem solving.
13. Encourage shared tasks.
    a. Who can lead?
    b. Who can be involved?
14. Provide for a safe environment
    a. For students.
    b. For staff.
15. Plan celebrations/recognitions—large and small.
    a. For success of the school goals
    b. For staff accomplishments
    c. For student achievement and attendance
    d. Establish joyous traditions.
    e. Just because
    f. Publically
    g. In Writing
    h. With Parties
16. Encourage storytelling.
    a. What are the traditions?
    b. What is going well? Why?
    c. Who is a hero? Why?
    d. What was a surprise in your classroom that led to increased student learning?
    e. How have you changed this year?
    f. Often
    g. About the past
    h. About the present

SOME BOOKS, ARTICLES, AND WEBSITES TO ESTABLISH A CULTURE OF HIGH ACHIEVEMENT

Drolet , Bonita, and Deborah Turner. *Building a bridge to success: From program improvement to excellence.* Lanham, MD: Rowman & Littlefield. 2010, p.122–126.
Harvey, T. R., W. L. Bearley, and S. M. Corkrum. *The practical decision maker: A handbook for decision making and problem solving in organizations.* Lancaster, PA: Technomic Publishing Company, Inc. 1997.

Harvey, Thomas, and Bonita Drolet. *Building teams building people, characteristics of effective teams survey.* Lanham, MD: Rowman & Littlefield. 2006.

Jerald, Craig. *School culture: The hidden curriculum.* Reading Rockets. December 2006. Retrieved from http://www.readingrockets.org/article/26095/.

Kruse, S. D., and K. S. Louis. *Building strong school cultures: A guide to leading change.* Thousand Oaks, CA: Corwin Press. 2009, p. 68–71.

Phillips, G. *Classroom Rituals for at risk learners.* Vancouver, BC: EduServ, British Columbia School Trustees Publishing. 1996.

Tschannen-Moran, Megan. "Moran's scale." Retrieved from http://mxtsch.people .wm.edu/research_tools.php.

Wagner and Masden-Copas. *School culture triage survey and audit date.*

West Ed's Healthy Kids School Climate Survey. Retrieved from http://www.wested. org/chks/pdf/scs_flyer_04.pdf.

Chapter Three

Vision and Values

> There is no more powerful engine driving an organization toward excellence and long-range success than an attractive, worthwhile, and achievable vision of the future, widely shared.
>
> —Burt Nanus

The eagle is the symbol of America. So should it be the symbol of all good leadership.

There are three characteristics of eagles that are particularly germane: 1) the eagle can see its target from miles away (hence the term "eagle eye"); 2) it continues to fly until it reaches its destination; and 3) it flies through rain, snow, or strong winds until it arrives at its destination.

So too should it be with good leadership. An effective leader should be able to have a far and near vision. He should keep going no matter what blocks his way—no matter what travails he has in his path. Finally he should keep going until he reaches his final goal.

These are the hallmarks of leadership—vision and persistence. The leader should stand for something and be willing to give her all for that something.

The principles of vision in a high-achieving environment are the following:

A CLEAR VISION IS A GOOD VISION

You can have a vision for an organization but if it's muddled, unclear, vague or unreadable, then it's as if you had no vision at all. As Nanus (1992) defines vision, it is "a realistic, credible, attractive future for your organization." Note that he said "realistic" and "credible." He might have added "clear" to this list

of objectives. We have seen many vision statement that are simply too vague
to carry the organization forward. They need to be realistic—capable of being
achieved—but far reaching so you have to stretch to achieve them.

It has become almost hackneyed to say an organization needs a vision.
Everyone buys into this. But it is a truism that EFFECTIVE leaders:

1. Have their vision statements,
2. Renew their vision statement every five years,
3. Clarify the difference between a mission and vision statement,
4. Have a readable, one-page vision statement, and
5. Use their vision statement as a guide to everyday action.

If you don't do any of the five things mentioned above, then you are an
ineffective leader and will be stuck in the status quo.

HIGH ACHIEVEMENT SHOULD BE A GOAL

To have high-achieving students, you must have high achievement as a goal
of your organization. In fact, you must have it as a number one goal! As described in chapter 4, high expectations for achievement are a necessary pre-
condition for any high-achieving environment. You must want achievement.
You must demand achievement of students, parents, teachers, administrators,
and staff. You must make it a prominent goal of your organization against
which all your actions and activities are gauged. You must develop and monitor all action plans that make achievement a reality.

But by "achievement" we don't mean just test scores. These are a part of
it. But it goes beyond this. How do you succeed in arts? in social networks?
in relationships? in learning about work? in problem solving and critical
thinking? in innovation and curiosity (Harvey, 2011)? All these and more
make up achievement. And you must make all of these things a goal of your
organization.

TO HAVE VISION, YOU'VE GOT TO HAVE VALUES

Vision statements are constantly monitored and changed. Values are not!
They are the bedrock of your organization. They are the fundamental operational principles that govern the direction of the organization's programs
and plans. Such principles as "Children come first," or "Programs focus on
developing a healthy mind and healthy body," or "Students are expected to

learn about cultural diversity within our community," are examples of tenet/value statements.

I remember working with a middle school that was toxic. People didn't work together because they had no direction. They fought over the smallest things. Most teachers didn't like being there and left as soon as they could. By the way, the majority of teachers were graduates of that middle school. They were dedicated to the school but not to each other.

We went in there and talked about the values they held. They formed a list of 11 values (tenets) they commonly subscribed to and we held them to these tenets. We formed a shared vision statement and some behavioral norms. They discovered that they had a lot in common. They began to work together. They began to turn around the school. The road wasn't free of bumps but the culture became more positive.

We have found in our 40 years of experience with schools that schools that are toxic are turned into positive schools with:

1. Vision statements,
2. Tenet statements,
3. Norms.

Without a school staff confronting these three elements, executing statements of each and then living up to these principles, a staff cannot turn around from a toxic environment to a positive, high-achieving one.

THERE ARE FOUR ELEMENTS TO A VISION STATEMENT

A vision statement is future-oriented. It describes what the organization is to look like and how it will successfully fulfill its intents. A vision statement is an outgrowth of the organization's tenets. In portraying a future state, the vision statement sketches clients, services, and strategies. It is the focus on the horizon that all members of the organization keep in sight and constantly work toward.

Attributes of a vision:

1. It focuses on a better future.
2. It encourages hopes and dreams.
3. It appeals to common values.
4. It states positive outcomes.
5. It emphasizes the strength of a unified group.
6. It uses word pictures, images, and metaphors.
7. It communicates enthusiasm and kindles excitement.

A vision is not:

1. A mission statement,
2. A simple statement of what is,
3. Boring and unimaginative,
4. Written but not used.

Therefore, the four elements of a vision statement are:

1. Desired future state: What does your organization want to look like five years from now?
2. Clientele served: Do you want to change who you are currently serving? Do you want to expand or retract from the current clientele?
3. Services provided: Do you want to redesign current general services, such as providing adult education, offering continual professional development, introducing cutting-edge technology, or offering global services?
4. Major strategies: Often confused with number 3, these are more specific in nature. Do you want every member of the team to have the opportunity to individualize professional development? Do you want to offer specific leadership possibilities?

STRATEGIC PLANNING IS THE
OPERATIONAL VERSION OF YOUR VISION

The way you implement your vision is through strategic planning. According to John Bryson (1995), strategic planning is "a disciplined effort to produce fundamental decisions and actions that shape and guide what an organization is, what it does, and why it does it."

Strategic planning helps an organization look at the long term, clarify future direction/vision, and develop a coherent and defensible basis for decision making. Organizations working from a strategic plan reach decisions in light of future consequences, establish sound priorities, and develop effective strategies. As a bonus, strategic planning helps team members solve major organizational problems, improve organizational performance, deal effectively with rapidly changing circumstances, strengthen expertise, and build teamwork. With the prospect of all these worthwhile results, is it not time to initiate strategic planning in your organization?

The following is an example of a vision statement.

The La Puente Valley Regional Occupational Program (LVROP) will be the leading ROP program in the state of California. This cooperative effort of the four school districts of Walnut Valley, Rowland, Bassett, and Hacienda–La Puente will be known for its regional collaboration and client centeredness. The LVROP will be seen as a lighthouse for innovation and a beacon for new technologies.

In order to serve the diverse student body of the future, there will be vocational offerings and programs for very different student populations – such groups as college-bound students, job-bound students, special education students, multicultural groups and gender groups there will be programs for students 16 years and older, both traditional and nontraditional, and for those previously served and those underserved.

The LVROP will provide pre-service and in-service vocational programs in all major vocational and technical areas, including but not limited to: computer technology and service, retail sales, animation, hospitality services, animal care, cosmetology, robotics, energy services, automotive care and the like.

In providing knowledge and job skill in these areas, it will also prepare students to be adaptive and resourceful in a fast changing vocational/technological world. To aid students in their successful transition to job placement and/or advanced vocational training, the LVROP will provide significant career guidance, placement services, business partnerships and cooperative (2+2) programs with other educational institutions.

The vision for the La Puente Valley Regional Occupational Program will be one of excitement, excellence and respect. Fully integrated into the educational life of the member districts, vocational education will be seen as one of the hallmarks and prides of the Walnut Valley, Rowland, Bassett, and Hacienda-La Puente School Districts.

Example 3.1.   Vision Statement

Steps in Strategic Planning

1. Form an appropriate team
2. Establish a plan to plan
3. Gather appropriate data

    a. SWOT analysis (strengths, weaknesses, opportunities, and threats that face the organization)

    b. External expectations

    c. Internal expectations

    d. Forecasts about the future

    e. Analysis of the present

    f. Analysis of the past

    g. Competitor profile

4. Develop tenets
5. Create a strategic vision statement
6. Examine current programs
7. Develop new programs
8. Identify strategic issues and needs
9. Formulate strategies for managing issues and programs
10. Devise action plans to manage issues and programs
11. Perform financial projections
12. Review feasibility of strategic vision
13. Monitor progress
14. Adjust the plan as needed

You do these plans with both a one-year and five-year focus. You then live out your plan because it is a blueprint for your high-achieving environment.

This is fine in theory. But I remember working with a high school on team building. Along the way they said that they had done a strategic plan and I asked to see it. After some effort they finally found a copy of it. While they did "strategic planning," it looked nothing like what it should. There was no vision statement—just a generic mission statement. There were three pages of pap and a list of things they wanted to get done in the future.

Clearly, this was neither specific nor focused enough to qualify as a strategic plan. But they had one. This kind of plan is worse than no plan at all. They deluded themselves into believing that they had one.

You've got to follow these steps or others like them, and have a specific and focused plan to guide your future. Then you've got to do it!

ALL CONSTITUENTS MUST BUY INTO THE VISION

In the February 17, 2012 episode of *Undercover Boss*, a TV series, the president of Checkers/Rally is seen talking proudly about his vision for the organization and how all the employees buy into this vision. But when he goes undercover into his fast food stores he finds that his manager isn't trained, doesn't know the vision that all employees will be treated with respect, and his service to customers is well under par. What a surprise he got!

Would we find the same if we all could be undercover bosses and discover how our people are carrying out our vision, or if they even know what the vision of the organization is?

Well, there are four ways that you could ensure that your constituents buy into the vision of the organization.

1. They have a hand in constructing the vision initially. Nothing achieves investment like participation. The teachers, the staff, the students, and the parents must be involved in a vision-setting exercise such as the one included later in this chapter.
2. Employees must be able to paraphrase accurately the vision. They must know the key words. They must know what is expected of them. They must be prepared to live out the vision.
3. Everyone must review it periodically, at least once a year. Collectively they must give input on how it's working and whether it needs to be re-vised.
4. Success must be measured against vision. There is an old saying: "What is evaluated, gets done." If you want your vision statement to be a living, breathing document, then you must monitor and assess its achievement.

In these ways you get your constituents to buy into the vision of the organization. When there's buy in, there is achieving of the vision. When a high-achieving environment is part of the vision, then you get a high-achieving environment.

These are the six principles that lead to vision:

1. A clear vision is a good vision.
2. High achievement should be a goal.
3. To have a vision, you've got to have values.
4. Four elements to a vision statement.
5. Strategic planning is the operational version of your vision.
6. All constituents must buy into the vision.

PRACTICAL SUGGESTIONS

These are some practical suggestions to implement vision:

Construct a Vision Statement
   • Have each participant write a futures letter, a letter that describes the organization hence. An example of this is to write a potential doctoral

student a letter describing why your doctoral program is the best one for the student.

- While they are writing the futures letter, put up four flip charts in the front of the room; write a different heading on each of the flip charts:
  1. Future state
  2. Client served
  3. Services provided
  4. Strategies to deliver service
- Have volunteers read their letters.
- As letters are read, you and/or your helpers record on each flip chart appropriate descriptors from their letters. For example, if a letter contains a future state, put it on the appropriate chart.
- When all letters are read (or at least as many as want to share) review the contents of each chart and see what it says about vision.
- The leader then writes a potential vision statement (like the one in Example 3.1).
- The group reviews and edits.
- Finally, the group gives it a final edit and approves it.
  1. Review the vision statement four times a year to see if you are doing it.
  2. Construct tenet/value statements.

Tenets are fundamental, operational principles that govern the direction of the organization's programs and plans. They establish the focus through which programs, products, and processes would be filtered prior to any decision. Tenets are usually composed of seven to ten statements of principle that drive the organization.

Without a strong belief in common tenets, values, or guiding principles, it is difficult for a team to flourish. Developing these belief statements takes time and talking. With a facilitator, use the following process:

1. Begin with each member of the team determining four to six of the organization's beliefs from the individual's perspective.
2. Place the team members in pairs to share their individual beliefs and come to consensus on six of the beliefs.
3. Form groups of four team members and repeat step 2.
4. Post the results of each group.
5. Have members place like beliefs together using an affinity chart or snow cards.
6. Come to consensus on the eight to ten beliefs that will guide your organization.

Bryant Ranch School is an example of a values statement:

Bryant Ranch School

Value Statements

- A positive and caring environment promotes intellectual curiosity, encourages creativity, and provides a balance between team work and independence.
- Promoting high self-esteem is the foundation for all school programs.
- Students and staff pride themselves in putting forth their best efforts.
- There is a strong sense of community awareness and responsibility.
- Students are provided opportunities to learn about and appreciate the cultural diversity within our community.
- Cooperation among staff, parents, and students encourages open communication and mutual support.
- Learning is celebrated as a lifelong experience.
- Students are recognized for striving towards academic success and appropriate behavior.
- Programs are provided that meet individual student needs.
- School-wide programs focus on developing a healthy mind and healthy body.
- Everyone is special.

CATCH THE SPIRIT AT BRYANT RANCH

Example 3.2. Values Statement

SOME BOOKS, ARTICLES AND WEBSITES TO SUPPORT VISION

Bennis, Warren, and Burt Nanus. *Leaders: Strategies for taking charge*. New York: Harper & Row. 2003.

Bilanech, Bud. *Using Values to Turn a Vision Into Reality*. 2000.

Broullitte, Liane. *Charter schools: Lessons in school reform in topics in educational leadership*. Lawrence Erlbaum Assocs. 2009.

Bryson, John. *Strategic planning for public and non profit organizations*. San Francisco: Jossey-Bass. 1995.

Cartwright, Taluka, and David Baldwin. *Communicating your vision*. Greensboro, NC: Center for Creative Leadership. 2006.

Deal, Terrence, and Peterson, Kent. *Shaping school culture*. San Francisco: Jossey-Bass. 2009.

Harvey, Thomas. *21st century schools*. La Verne, CA: EPIC Monograph. 2011.

Kouzes, James, and Barry Posner. *The leadership challenge*. San Francisco: Jossey-Bass. 1987.

Nanus, Burt. *Visionary leadership*. San Francisco: Jossey-Bass. 1992.

Pielstick, Dean. "Beyond vision: The transforming leader." 2006. Retrieved from www.cha.nav.edu/pielstick 2006.

Southwest Educational Development Laboratory. "Vision, leadership and change." *Issues . . . about Change.* 2(3).

Weiss, Alan. *Good enough isn't enough.* Amacom Book. 2000.

Chapter Four

High Expectations

High achievement always takes place in the framework of high expectation.

—Charles F. Kettering, American engineer and inventor

The need for educators to have high expectations for student achievement has been studied and discussed for years. The results of these studies do not clarify a direct relationship between an educational leader proclaiming "high expectations" and increased student achievement. However, the studies do show a relationship when leaders and classroom teacher leaders establish a climate of high expectations by their actions (Green, 2005).

Leadership that seeks to inspire and establish a climate of high expectations or rigor for all students intentionally encourages actions that support the outcome of higher student achievement. The principles of establishing high expectations that lead to intentions of action and yield a high-achieving environment are:

LOW EXPECTATIONS EQUAL LOW ACHIEVEMENT

To some this may seem like a negative principle, however it is the first principle all educational leaders should grasp if their intent is to positively impact student achievement. In 2004 President George W. Bush coined the term "the soft bigotry of low expectations" in his speech supporting the No Child Left Behind (NCLB) legislation. The NCLB legislation started an avalanche of controversy and debate regarding the role of testing, teachers teaching to the test, and the impracticality of applying the same standards to all children.

That debate continues today, but the role of low expectations continues to impact student performance in classrooms across our nation. The National Education Association (NEA at http://www.nea.org/home/1052.htm) has published a number of articles regarding student achievement and the phenomena of the "achievement gap." One of the top reasons reported by the NEA for not closing the achievement gap in public education is schoolwide low expectation.

The evidence is overwhelming that low expectations yield low results. A study by Delpit (1995) found a connection between low teacher expectations and students' ability to achieve. He felt strongly about this link as evidenced by his statement, "It is hard to believe that these children can possibly be successful after their teachers have . . . so much negative indoctrination . . . . [T]here is a tendency to assume deficits in students rather than to locate and teach to strengths" (Delpit, 1995, p. 172).

In a number of studies done at Stanford with African American students, the findings indicated that the negative stereotypes and low expectations of African American students negatively impacted the ability to perform on standardized tests. A longitudinal study was conducted by the National Center for Education Statistics. Starting in 2002, this study focused on a nationally representative group of high school sophomores and then followed them through their high school careers.

This study resulted in a breadth of information about student test achievement, attitudes, and experiences. One of the important findings was the evidence that low expectations do have an impact on student achievement.

If there is any hint of excuse for lowering the student achievement expectation for any type or group of students, then the quest to improve student achievement will be negatively impacted. Even the innocent or unintentional forms of low expectation can lead to the "soft bigotry" that negatively impacts student achievement.

This is illustrated by a recent blog titled "Low Expectations Kill." This blog was about a parent's experience with a well-known charter school that operates different schools in the greater Phoenix area. When they opened one close to his home, the father enrolled his son with high hopes. He describes his disappointment in the level of achievement his son experienced while attending and attributes the problem to low expectations. He points out that when this school was opened the mistake that they made was labeling the school "Low Income."

Those two words, which often denote low expectations for achievement to some people, took a formula that was wildly successful and a body of families eager to support the venture and poisoned the minds of the majority of the teaching staff, according to the father's account. He goes on to explain that the "kicker" was many of the students were from an affluent minority, yet the labeling of the school "low income" established a dangerous mind-set of teachers and administrators for lowering expectations.

The evidence was clear for this father that low expectations do yield low achievement.

HIGH EXPECTATIONS CAN BE A
SELF-FULFILLING PROPHECY

Zig Ziglar, an internationally acclaimed motivational speaker, wrote a book titled *See You At The Top*. In his chapters on relationships with others he develops a narrative based on research studies and anecdotes to build a strong case about the way leaders should see others. He concludes with "the way you see people is the way you treat them and the way you treat them is the way they often become" (Ziglar, 2000).

This belief that expectations based on how we see and treat people can make a difference for others was recognized by the poet Goethe over three hundred years ago when he penned: "When you take a man as he is, you make him worse. When you take a man as he can be, you make him better." If you're looking for a more recent support, Kati Haycock (2012) has consistently written and advocated for educational leaders to promote high expectations as a very important component of raising student achievement.

Ovid has commonly described this phenomenon as the Pygmalion Effect in one of his narratives in Greek mythology. George Bernard Shaw published his play *Pygmalion* in 1916 based on the phenomena of the influence of expectations on a person's behavior. This play was later transformed into the musical adaptation, Academy Award winning best picture *My Fair Lady*.

You may recall the main character, the Cockney flower girl Eliza Doolittle, and her explanation of how high expectations (the way we see people) translate into behavior when she states: "You see, really and truly, apart from the things anyone can pick up (the dressing and the proper way of speaking and so on), the difference between a lady and a flower girl is not how she behaves, but how she's treated. I shall always be a flower girl to Professor Higgins, because he always treats me as a flower girl, and always will; but I know I can be a lady to you, because you always treat me as a lady, and always will."

Over the years there have been educators who expressed some doubt about the impact of high expectations and self-fulfilling prophecy despite the many scientific studies that have been published supporting the phenomena.

In 1968 the findings of a now classic experiment in the sociology of education, was published in a book by Robert Rosenthal (Harvard professor) and Leonore Jacobson (Elementary School Principal) titled *Pygmalion in the Classroom: Teacher Expectation and Pupils' Intellectual Development* (1992). The premise of their study was that the higher expectations teachers have for their students do positively influence the behavior of those students.

They randomly selected 20 percent of students (called "growth spurters" by Rosenthal & Jacobson) at an elementary school and told their teachers that these students had great intellectual potential and should be expected to excel in their academic accomplishments during the school year.

Well guess what? These randomly selected students with a wide span of verified IQs did show significant increases compared to the other 80 percent that were not labeled as having greater intellectual potential. Further, when their teachers were asked to rank the intellectual and social characteristics, they ranked these students as "more intellectually curious, happier, and having less need for social approval."

There have been some critiques of the statistical foundation of the Rosenthal-Jacobson study over the years, even some by Rosenthal. However, there are now over 400 studies on the self-fulfilling impact of high expectations as well as a number of meta-analyses of studies that provide evidence regarding the importance of high expectations on student achievement, leaving little doubt about the importance of the self-fulfilling prophecy impact.

A key theme from these studies is the relationship of teachers' high expectations and what seem to me unintended, yet observable, verbal and nonverbal behaviors that have been documented as contributing to the students' achieving at a higher level. These behaviors can run the gamut of unintended encouraging facial/body language when asking a question to the actual planning/implementation of instruction and use of instructional strategies.

The impact of educational leaders' and teachers' strong belief in high expectations for all students and their ability to succeed is well established. Stephen Farr, Chief Knowledge Officer for Teach For America and author of *Teaching as Leadership* (2010), has studied data regarding student achievement with an eye on determining what differentiates the "pedigree teacher" from those who are less effective in positively impacting student achievement. One of the main differences found by Farr was that the "pedigree teachers" develop and maintain high expectations for their students.

When Donna Carrier, the only teacher in Kentucky to be recognized by the U.S. Department of Education as the "No Child Left Behind American Star of Teaching" received her citation, it stated, "She has such high expectations for all her children." These "high expectations" resulted in an increase in migrant school student population social studies proficiency from 58.5 percent to 96 percent! The development of the culture of high expectations for all students as a driver for increased achievement is a consistent finding in educational research over the years (Newmann and Wehlage, 1995).

The way you see your students and maintain high expectations will impact the way you treat them and, therefore, the way they will eventually behave. The role of establishing and promoting the concept that all students should be perceived and believed to be "growth spurters" starts at the top and does result in identifiable, higher student achievement.

HIGH EXPECTATIONS NEED HIGH SUPPORT

It is important to encourage others to have high student expectations but you cannot expect great student achievement results by just espousing the importance of high expectations. A strong culture of high expectations is essential for high student achievement but does not by itself produce the kind of behavioral change in leaders, teachers, and ultimately in students that leads to high student achievement as illustrated in the "High Expectations Can Be a Self-fulfilling Prophecy" principle section without strong support.

So many educators forget those early days when they were first hired fresh out of a college credentialing program and inspired to teach all children and help them find their place in the world. Then the reality set in. They had the title "teacher" and the responsibilities and were now given document after document, notebook after notebook, regarding curriculum, system process/ policy, and requirements for tenure. The reality then sets in and the high expectations can be dimmed without high support.

I am reminded of my old football-coaching days when I think about the relationship of high expectations and high support. When I first began my high school football-coaching career I would espouse high expectations for individual player performance as well as team performance.

However, in the first year of coaching I was basically learning on the job and devoted most of my time to my understanding of the role and strategies of becoming a football coach. The result was less support of the players for developing the skills needed to reach the high expectations I espoused. The teams' record at the end of the year was a reflection of this phenomenon: 2 wins and 6 losses.

The next year I had gained more knowledge/strategies by attending coaching clinics and networking with successful coaches so I was better able to focus on implementing the skill building and instruction for my players that would actually allow them to reach their potential and the high expectations. The second year we had a 7–2 season.

In the third year we won the league championship. High expectations alone were not enough, but combined with high support for those high expectations the ability to succeed was unleashed.

The "game" of achieving high student success is more complex than my football analogy and gaining more knowledge/strategies by attending clinics and networking did not, in itself, ensure success. However, it does help illustrate the point about high expectations' need to be combined with high support.

Robert Marzano (2010) recognizes the need for high expectations accompanied by high support in his recent article in *Educational Leadership* titled "High Expectations for All." In this article he addresses the importance of high expectations but makes the important point that, subtle as it may be, teachers can foster lower expectations for students based on a number of factors such as student behavior, race, or perception of past teachers. He points out that it takes focused support (actions) to change the behaviors of teachers to yield greater student success.

Marzano (2010) stresses that helping to communicate high expectations can be supported as an instructional strategy using the following four steps:

1. Identify students for whom you have low expectations.
2. Identify similarities in students.
3. Identify differential treatment of low-expectancy students.
4. Treat low-expectancy and high-expectancy students the same.

High-level support from policy makers and administrators is a key to how we bring about significant change in behaviors that will eventually impact high student achievement. The California Department of Education (CDE) published a report titled "Taking Center Stage—Act II" (TCSII) in 2011 and stated,

> Schools which establish high expectations for all youth—and give them the support necessary to achieve them—have high rates of academic success. These schools also have lower rates of problem behaviors such as dropping out, alcohol and other drug abuse, teen pregnancy, and delinquency than other schools. Conveying positive and high expectations in a classroom and school environment occurs at several levels ("Taking Center Stage," 2011).

The "levels" of support can and should occur at the federal, state and local levels. It does begin with a well-communicated vision/belief from the top down that all students can achieve academic success. It is then translated into actions such as the development of curriculum and teaching strategies that address a broad range of learning styles to support student learning; a culture of clear communication regarding high expectations for all facets of student engagement; and budget decision making that is focused on a clear outcome of higher student achievement.

HIGH EXPECTATIONS NEED TO BE
PERCEIVED IN THE SYSTEM

The first three principles previously discussed are important principles for fostering high student achievement in any school system. They are also precursors that lead us to the final principle that high expectations need to be perceived in the system.

A lot has been written on the "systems-thinking approach" that has emerged from the work of MIT professor Jay Forrester in 1956. A student of systems-thinking theory can easily get lost in the many theoretical frameworks, constructs, and detailed diagram simulations of systems thinking in action.

A recent travel experience might help illustrate the importance of understanding the organization as a system that can be influenced and derailed by one of its many parts. I was scheduled to fly into Ontario Airport from Sky Harbor the other day for an important meeting that started at 11:00 a.m. I was booked on a flight that was scheduled to land in Ontario at 10:15 a.m. Having made this trip many times I was confident all would go well and I could easily make the 11 a.m. meeting. However, the flight from Phoenix to Ontario originated out of New Orleans. It seems one of the flight crew was late arriving at the airport in New Orleans and delayed the flight.

The next leg of the flight was Chicago. Although the crew member's tardiness only delayed the original flight 15 minutes, in Chicago the problem was compounded because now it was delayed at the gate because other flights were ahead of that plane in the take-off order at O'Hare. Therefore, the flight arrived in Phoenix 35 minutes late. By the time it was loaded and on the tarmac for take-off it was delayed again because of other planes scheduled ahead for take-off.

Yes, I was over an hour late for that meeting. The small 15-minute delay caused by the flight crew member resulted in a one hour late flight given the impact on the entire system.

The flight illustration is applicable to how the systems view can impact public education. The view that we can control our district or school is misleading just like my belief that I could depend on the plane schedule. Margaret Wheatley (1999), in writing about systems thinking and public education states,

> We are confronted daily by events and outcomes that surprise us. Nothing moves slowly enough for us to make sense of the world using any analytic process we were taught. And the complexity of modern systems cannot be understood by separating issues into neat boxes and diagrams. In a complex system, it is impossible to find simple causes that explain our problems, or to know who to blame. A messy tangle of relationships has given rise to these unending crises. We need a different worldview to guide us in this new world of continuous change and intimately connected systems that reach around the globe.

For our purpose, the important take away is that systems-thinking focuses on how the organization can be influenced and behavior can be changed by the many "parts" of the system versus the older organizational behavioral dynamic that emphasized a singular focus within the organization as the key to bringing about a desired change. Just like the flight story, educational leaders should employ a systems-thinking approach that causes them to view the many different parts of their very human organization.

As Margaret Wheatley (1999) stated, "In a complex system, it is impossible to find simple causes that explain our problems, or to know who to blame." Systems-thinking educational leaders understand the importance that many different parts of their organization have on student achievement and will seek to lead meaningful change across departments, schools, and teams to bring about higher student achievement.

I believe the current explosion of Professional Learning Communities (PLC) literature, approach, and attempted conversion of schools across our nation are really an example of the systems-thinking approach to organizational change. However, the danger of the PLC movement was clearly stated by DuFour in 2004: that the whole PLC movement could run the risk "of losing all meaning" because "people use this term to describe every imaginable combination of individuals with an interest in education—a grade-level teaching team, a school committee, a high school department, an entire school district, a state department of education, a national professional organization and so on."

The vast number of studies, articles, and books written about PLCs and producing high student achievement produce a common theme that supports the need for systems thinking as the approach to high student achievement. The different constructs underlying PLCs are a form of the systems approach.

Parrett and Budge's book published by ASCD is directed at turning high-poverty schools into high-performing schools and their findings support the principle that high expectations need to be systemic—perceived and acted upon throughout the school. They challenge school leaders to recognize that there is no "one size fits all" solution and that school leaders willing to focus their efforts on becoming a high-performing school do and will be successful in raising student achievement.

In closing this chapter, the work of Ronald R. Edmonds in establishing the effective schools movement significantly supports the power of high expectations for high achievement for all students. Edmonds (1979) was unwavering in his conviction that schools could be changed or reformed to become effective for all students. He strongly supported the notion that high expectations do yield high-achieving students.

Unfortunately, his famous quote from an article in *Educational Leadership* (October, 1979) is still as stinging now as it was 30 years ago: "It seems to me, therefore, that what is left of this discussion are three declarative statements: (a) We can, whenever and wherever we choose, successfully teach all children whose schooling is of interest to us; (b) We already know more than we need to do that; and (c) Whether or not we do it must finally depend on how we feel about the fact that we haven't so far" (p. 23).

If we truly want to look back one day with the ability to say we have fundamentally changed our schools so all children can and do achieve, then we can start improving student achievement with the four principles for having high expectations.

Therefore, the following four principles lead to high expectations:

- Low expectations equal low achievement.
- High expectations can be a self-fulfilling prophecy.
- High expectations need high support.
- High expectations need to be perceived in the system.

PRACTICAL SUGGESTIONS

1. Establish goals for high expectations across the curriculum including music, arts, and PE.
2. Use key words, phrases, and/or metaphors so they become memorable to all members of the organization.
3. Ask the difficult question, "Do teachers and staff members believe all students can learn?" If unable to clearly answer "yes," then consider key ongoing professional development and support that will foster behavioral changes that reflect a belief in high expectations for all students.
4. Define what you want for high expectations—academic and behavioral—that supports and communicates a "no excuses" attitude with staff, students, and parents.
5. Provide training and resources for all staff members that support the vision that high expectations result in high achievement, such as:
   - Student-centered curriculum
   - Variety of instructional strategies to meet the learning needs of all students
   - Effective classroom management strategies as well as classroom environment.
6. Celebrate student achievement at all levels—classroom, departments, school- and/or districtwide, and communitywide.
7. Purposively share and encourage others to share stories of student success that was an outgrowth of high expectations vision.

8. Have teachers share how high expectations have changed their teaching and students' learning.
9. Include your sports coaches in the discussion about the importance of high expectations. Ask them to share how the vision of high expectations can result in success on the field.

SOME BOOKS, ARTICLES AND WEBSITES TO SUPPORT HIGHER EXPECTATIONS

Delpit, L. *Other people's children: Cultural conflict in the classroom*. New York: The New Press. 1995.

Edmonds, R. "Effective schools for the urban poor." *Educational Leadership*. 1979: 37(1), pp. 15–27.

Farr, S. *Teaching as leadership: The highly effective teacher's guide to closing the achievement gap*. San Francisco: Jossey-Bass. 2010.

Green, R. L. *Expectations: How teacher expectations can increase student achievement and assist in closing the achievement gap*. Columbus, OH: McGraw-Hill. 2005.

Haycock, K. "Closing the achievement gap for native students." *The Huffington Post*. July 12, 2012. Retrieved September 19, 2012, from: http://www.huffingtonpost.com/kati-haycock/achievement-gap-native-students_b_1672247.html.

Haycock, Kati, "Education Trust leader Kati Haycock addresses Lesley Leadership Council." October 19, 2012. Retrieved from http://news.lesley.edu/2012/10/education-trust-leader-kati-haycock-addresses-lesley-leadership-council.shtml.

Livingston, J. S. "Pygmalion in management (HRB Classic)." *Harvard Business Review*. January, 2003: pp. 5–12.

Marzano, R. J. "High expectations for all." *Educational Leadership*. September 2010: 68(1), pp. 82–84. Retrieved from http://www.ascd.org/publications/educational-leadership/sept10/vol68/num01/High-Expectations-for-All.aspx.

Newmann, F., and G. Wehlage. *Successful school restructuring*. Madison, WI: Center on Organization and Restructuring of Schools. 1995.

Rosenthal, R., and L. Jacobson. *Pygmalion in the classroom* (Expanded ed.). New York: Irvington. 1992.

"Taking center stage—Act II." California Department of Education (CDE). 2011. Retrieved August, 2012, from http://www.cde.ca.gov/ci/gs/mg/cefmgtcsii.asp.

Wheatley, M. J. "Bringing schools back to life: Schools as living systems." Excerpted from *Creating successful school systems: Voices from the university, the field, and the community*. Christopher-Gordon Publishers. September 1999. Retrieved September 14, 2012, from http://www.margaretwheatley.com/articles/lifetoschools.html.

Ziglar, Z. *See you at the top* (2nd ed.). Gretna, LA: Pelican Publishing Company, Inc. 2000.

Chapter Five

Love and Passion

You've got to love your work.

—Anonymous

For a long and enjoyable career, it has been said that you have to love your work. But more than that, we would argue that you have to demonstrate love and passion to have a truly successful career. Without these two qualities, you are going through the motions; or you are faking it. The same is true of schools. Without these qualities you cannot model a zest for learning that is important to a high-achieving environment.

In particular, you need to exemplify the following principles:

LOVE THE PEOPLE YOU WORK WITH

You need to love the children you serve and the teachers who do the work. In fact, you need to love the custodians, the aides, the parents, and the classified staff.

My wife was an elementary principal who loved kids. When she had a particularly hard day, she had to get out to the playground to get a "kid break." She loved hugging them and talking to them. She loved being with them. One day when all the kids submitted a drawn picture of her, she was depicted as a woman with her arms spread out receiving all the kids. She expressed love. She got love.

Contrary to that, I knew a director of a senior citizen facility and he hated seniors. He avoided them and ignored their needs. He set a low-service environment. He was not the leader you would want to be like.

You need to love the people you seek to serve. Exemplifying this was Juan, who served dinner at a restaurant with zest and grins. He loved being a waiter. The food was only mediocre. But he was splendid. We loved the restaurant. Everyone did. Which would you rather be—the senior citizen community director or Juan?

You need to love all the people who do the work. It is hard to be collaborative with people who you don't like or trust. You need to exult in their achievements and weep with them in their failures. In fact, I knew a dean who often said, "This university would be wonderful if wasn't for the faculty." He didn't like the faculty and it showed. He lasted only two years. Eventually the faculty got even with him. He set a toxic environment.

You can't last long or achieve much without loving the faculty—or the custodians—or whoever does the work.

Relationships are the key to good management. Everywhere we look, good relationships are critical to effective leadership. We talk about the components of relationships—team building, collaborative decision making, effective change management, successful conflict resolution, and on and on.

Relationships are everything. And the key to relationships is love. You have got to love the people you're with by encouraging the heart. "Love of their products, their people, their customers, then work—this may just be the best-kept secret of exemplary leadership" (Kouzes and Posner, 1988, p. 13). Love of the people you work with leads you to love of your work.

LOVE THE WORK

Imagine working at a job you hate. You dread going into work. You can't wait until the day is over. Will you inspire kids? Will you demonstrate and model passion? Of course not! You have to love your work.

You've got to love the teaching-learning process or you will become quickly bored with the work of education. And bored people are not very good leaders. But more than this, if you are bored with the work you do, you will eventually demonstrate ennui and this modeling cannot help but make your followers bored.

When I was made a dean at my university, I continued to teach. I loved the teaching process and could not imagine doing without it. I just loved my work. Juan just loved waiting on people. My wife loved doing the work of education.

But this is easier said than done. I fear that people are settling for just getting or keeping a job. In this prolonged economic downturn, many people are out of work. They take any job they can get, whether they love it or not. This bodes badly for many of our institutions. It is imperative that we have people who really want to be there. Loving the work you do is everything.

LOVE IS A SKILL

Love may be a feeling. If it is, that's wonderful. But what if it isn't? Do you quit? No!

Love is a skill. It is a set of behaviors you practice until you are good at it. Whether you are introverted or extroverted, naturally loving or shy, come from a loving family or not, you can still express the behaviors that make up love. You can ask people questions. You can listen intently to the answers. You can express empathy to others. You can give hugs or pats on the back. You can laugh with them. You can cry with them. You can demonstrate compassion with them. These are some of the behaviors of love. You don't have to be naturally or instinctively loving, as long as you express these behaviors.

Love is:

1. Asking
2. Listening
3. Empathizing
4. Hugging
5. Laughing or crying.

I remember a high school principal. He stayed in his office except for meetings. The staff assumed he just didn't care for them. The truth was that he was painfully shy. I encouraged him to walk around and just ask questions of everyone. He prepared his questions. After a while he became comfortable with questions, so he started to say emphatic responses. Then he practiced authentic laughing. He never got to hugging, but the staff saw him as "caring now." He just had to practice his skills of love.

Practice these behaviors and you'll become good at them.

BE A GOOD FINDER

In feedback theory, if you give someone discomforting feedback, they will change. If you give feedback that they expect, they will not change. The implication of this research is that if you want someone who is low performing to alter their behavior, you need to give him/her positive feedback. You need to catch him/her doing something well. On the other hand, you don't need to give high-performers feedback. You just need to celebrate their successes.

In either case you must concentrate on the positive. If you want to have a high-achieving environment, you need to be a good finder—particularly if you love the people you work with.

I had a poetry teacher in college, Dr. Ludwig. He was a classic good finder. Every time we suggested our interpretation of a poem, he found some aspects of our comments that were worthy of praise. He molded our opinions by praising what was good. I signed up for all his classes, even though I didn't care about poetry. I just loved hearing from this good finder and I did everything to live up to his standards.

Where you do the "good finding" is also important. You need to go to where the work is being actually done—the classroom, the halls, the cafeteria, the teachers' lounge, and so forth. The worst place is your office. Great leaders take the time to walk around—and celebrate successes.

BE OBVIOUS

It is important to model the way (Kouzes and Posner, 2003). Be obvious. Show empathically your love for the work and people you serve. If you're shy, fake it. The more obvious you are, the more they will get the point—love works.

We have a saying, "The message you send is the message you will receive." If you express dispassion for your work and a blasé attitude about students and teachers, then you get back an attitude of not-caring and ennui with the work they do. But if you send a message of love and passion, then it will infect all around you! Would you rather work in a loving environment or one that doesn't care?

Did you ever meet a fine craftsman who didn't love what he was doing? He was proud and didn't mind telling you how beautiful his work was. He/she is not humble. He is obvious with his passion. And we marvel at it. I lived in the same town as Sam Maloof, the renowned furniture artisan. He created great furniture and was not humble about it. He wouldn't sell you a piece unless you showed proper appreciation for it. He demonstrated a passion and ardor for his creations.

Be a craftsman of leadership. Show love and passion.

LOVE AND RESULTS

Love does matter in results. "Leaders who trigger emotional engagement release 400 percent more discretionary effort than those who trigger rational engagement" (Corporate Leadership Council, 2004). You can affect their minds and get some results. But affect their hearts and you'll reap four times the results. By expressing passion and love, you increase the likelihood of a high-achieving environment. And we all want high-achieving environments. Then why don't we?

In our academic preparation and training we are taught to think, to cogitate, to be logical. But we know that great teachers are loving and loved. They are not afraid to speak from the heart—to feel. Even the great ones who are gruff and demanding demonstrate a love of learning and a passion for the truth. Expressing feelings, expressing love, leads to greater results.

ESTABLISH RELATIONSHIPS

In a poll of workers, the five reasons people give for loving their jobs are:

1. The challenge
2. Great bosses
3. Great coworkers
4. Work that matters
5. Being employed.

Items 2 and 3 on this list express the appreciation for the people that they work with. The relationships. Relationships are everything! People who love their jobs don't remember the tasks they did or the paperwork they completed. They remember the people. When they retire, they miss great coworkers and bosses. Or they are relieved that they no longer have to work with lousy bosses or coworkers. When they look back upon their work life they remember the relationships, whether bad or good.

CAVEATS

Let me add some caveats about these principles.

First of all, you have to do them all. You can love the work but hate the teachers. You can love the students, but stay in your office all the time and hide out. You can love the people who do the work but not be a good finder. You have to do all of these things if you want to have a high-achieving environment. To do otherwise is to fail.

Secondly, you must at times express tough love. You sometimes have got to be critical and demanding but always with a high sense that they can do it and will do it. Jaime Escalante is a wonderful example of this quality. A teacher of calculus at Garfield High in Los Angeles, he taught his poor, immigrant students calculus so well that all passed the advanced placement test into college. In fact, ETS was so skeptical of this feat that they made the students retake the test; they were sure that there was fraud. But they all passed it a second time. How did he achieve this? He had a passion for calculus. He believed in his students. He hounded them and demanded much of them. He expressed love and tough love. And he established a high-achieving environment.

Brady Wilson expresses this conundrum so well when he said "Love challenges people to stretch to the point of tearing their muscles" (Wilson, 2010, p. 169). Love means to push people beyond their comfort zones.

I experienced this only too well when I suffered a severe stroke at age 51. I pitied myself and expected everyone else to follow suit. But, alas, my rehab nurses did not. They pushed me beyond my seeming breaking point. They hounded me. And to this day I thank them for showing me the eight months of tough love that allowed me to walk and talk again. They expressed more love than I deserved. I pitied myself. They loved me. In the end I'd rather have what they gave me than what I was willing to settle for. Tough love.

The following six principles lead to love and passion:

1. Love the people you work with.
2. Love the work.
3. Love is a skill.
4. Be a good finder.
5. Be obvious.
6. Establish relationships.

PRACTICAL SUGGESTIONS

These are some practical suggestions for implementing love and passion:

1. Create a picture book: Each year, put together a picture book of your staff. Have candid shots and group shots.
2. Practice skills of love: Practice every day one or more of these love skills:
   a. Asking
   b. Listening
   c. Empathizing
   d. Hugging
   e. Laughing or crying
3. Take kid breaks: At least twice a day take a 15–30 minute break and go out with the kids. You can play with them; you can hug them; or you can listen to them. Nothing says you love them like being with them. And it doesn't cost anything.

4. Make lounge visits: Go to where teachers congregate on their breaks or at lunchtime. Ask them questions and then listen to their answers. Go to where the custodians are and listen to them. You can find a wealth of information out this way. Go to wherever anyone works and talk to them. Schedule/visit twice a day.
5. Spend time: Spend time each day with a staff member to learn about them personally and professionally. Talk to them about things other than work.
6. Send notes: Send your employees a note twice a week. Celebrate their personal or professional milestones or accomplishments.
7. Fill out a "Love Form"

Week	Lounge Visits	Spend Time w/Employees	Correspondence to Employees
1		John Doe or Jane Doe	✓ Thank you note to Jill
2		Etc.	✓ Congratulations to Jim on birth of baby
3			
4			
5			
6			
7			
8			
9			
10			
*			
*			
*			
N			

Form 5.1. Love Form

SOME BOOKS AND ARTICLES TO
SUPPORT LOVE AND PASSION

Adams, John. *Miracles at work.* New London, CT: Life Without Limits Press. 2005.

Cashman, Kevin. *The pause principle*, San Francisco: Berrett-Koehler. 2012.

Corporate Leadership Council. *Driving performance and retention through employee engagement.* Washington, DC: Corporate Executive Board. 2004.

Fay, Jim, and David Funk. *Teaching with love and logic.* Golden, CO: Love and Logic Press. 1995.

Fletcher, Jerry. *Patterns of high performance.* San Francisco: Berrett-Koehler Publishers. 1993.

Gilman, Cheryl. *Doing the work you love.* Chicago: Contemporary Books. 1997.

Jobs, Steve. Stanford Commencement Address by Steve Jobs. *Stanford UMV News, Stanford Report.* June 14, 2005.

"Key to Business success: Love the work you do." 2011. Retrieved from Getoutfromunderyourbusiness.com.

Kouzes, James, and Barry Posner. *Encouraging the heart.* San Francisco: Jossey-Bass. 2003.

Toms, Michael, and Justine Toms. *True work.* New York: Crown Publishing. 1998.

Tracy, Brian. *Maximum qchievement.* New York: BPS Books. 2010.

Wilson, Brady. *Love challenges all.* 2010.

Chapter Six

Focus on Learning
and Academic Rigor

America's economic and social well-being is increasingly dependent upon the capacity of our public education system to prepare all students for college and high-performance careers. With almost 80 percent of today's fastest-growing jobs requiring some postsecondary education, all students—regardless of their race/ethnicity, gender, socioeconomic or disability status—need to complete an academically rigorous high school curriculum in order to be well-equipped for productive work and civic life.

—Pathways to College Network

While there are many types of achievement, this chapter is focused on academic learning and rigor. Academic rigor can be defined as the set of standards we set for our students and the expectations we have for them and ourselves. Rigor is much more than assuring that the course content is of sufficient difficulty. Rigor includes our basic philosophy of learning: We expect our students to demonstrate not only content mastery but applied skills and critical thinking about the disciplines being taught (Roueche 2002). With that being said, how rigorous are the curricula and expectations at your school? Your district?

The time has come to focus our attention on learning and academic rigor, because other countries have been doing so for years and the United States is on a downward spiral when compared to other developed nations. As we have moved solidly into an information society, we need young minds who know how to reason and think—not just recall knowledge on multiple choice tests—no matter how high level the questions seem to be. We need to be directing our attention to ensuring that students can think about every subject they encounter, research information, and then determine rationally what answers might apply to the problem posed.

Teachers who understand that knowledge is not test taking, but rather serious investigations into all angles of a subject, are promoting a focus on learning and academic rigor. They understand the principles discussed in this chapter.

STUDENT LEARNING IS THE CHIEF
RESPONSIBILITY OF EVERYONE

If you are the superintendent or a district office staff member, do you limit the number of meetings that pull the principal away from the main responsibility of being in the classroom? Are you on a campus at least once a week to see how your policies and procedures affect student learning and achievement?

If you are the principal of a school, you should be making learning the highest priority of your day. You can do this by making sure that you are visiting classrooms every day. Be sure that it is on your calendar, so something of less importance does not take precedence.

If you are a teacher, you need to structure your classroom to maximize student learning. That means having routines in place that minimize disruptions and maximize on-task learning time. Do the students in your room move from subject to subject with ease and within a few minutes if you are elementary? If you are a secondary teacher, does instruction and, more importantly, learning begin the minute students enter your room?

If you are a part of the wonderful support staff that is the glue that holds the school together, do you respond to teacher and student needs in a timely fashion? Are you there for them for special learning events? Is the custodian or plant manager aware of schedules so that disruptions do not impact student learning by occurring during key learning times? Is office staff aware of each teacher's schedule so an interruption won't occur just when a great point is being made that will ensure greater learning by the students?

Learning is everyone's responsibility—not just the teacher's, the parent's and the student's! We must all circle around those classrooms to ensure that learning time and the end result of greater academic achievement happen consistently for every student.

SET HIGH EXPECTATIONS FOR LEARNING

Oftentimes entering a classroom causes one to wonder: "What is going on here?" Students may be off task or roaming around the room. The teacher may be working with a small group and not looking up to see what is going on around the room.

Conversely, walking into a room with high expectations for learning and academic achievement, one sees a very different scene.

- The first thing you notice is that no one is off task! As you walk around the room and ask students what they are learning (not doing!), they are very clear on the learning intention and the outcomes needed to show they understand the concept presented.
- Students are focused on the learning, but also have a clear understanding of what to do when finished with the assigned task.
- The teacher may be working with a small group, but there is a system in place for students to ask a peer for help before going to the teacher.
- The teacher is visually watching the entire class as work proceeds with the small group.
- If the teacher is presenting a whole-group lesson, the students are also aware of the learning intention for the lesson and what they are expected to know at the end of instruction.
- Students are called on at random and if they cannot answer, they may ask a friend, but then are still responsible for responding. No one is let off the hook and everyone knows it! It is the classroom contract that students and teacher abide by all-day long. Students are expected to know the material presented in each learning intention and they know it! There is no vacillating about learning.

The students know in these classrooms that in order to achieve, they must stay focused, and the teacher knows that in order for students to achieve, expectations must be clearly spelled out and adhered to; no excuses!

COLLABORATE TO DETERMINE THE BEST THINKING

No one person has all of the answers; that is why collaboration is necessary in education for all students to achieve success. That is why it is a 21st century skill! Many schools across the nation are implementing professional learning communities, teacher learning communities, or just plain learning communities in order to bring together the best minds to help students succeed.

Whatever a teacher group is called, its express purpose is to discuss student achievement. Is student achievement happening? Why? Why not? What can be done to change the status quo? The old saying TEAM = Together Everyone Achieves More has never been more applicable than when applying it to educators working together to change the direction of a student's learning.

DEFINE RIGOR

How will we know what rigor is if we don't stop and define it for those who teach, those who observe, and those who learn. It is important to develop a set of best management practices for promoting academic excellence. It is important to have strategies for establishing instructional goals for academic excellence and ways for documenting progress toward these goals. And lastly, it is important to assess our current understanding of rigor in the classroom.

Many definitions of rigor abound. Primarily, the essential components of rigor are content acquisition, critical thinking, relevance, integration, application of concepts, long-term retention, and responsibility for classroom behavior for teachers and students.

Olympic Educational Services District #114 in Bremerton, Washington, came up with a great way to remember what is meant by "Academic Rigor" (www.oesd.wednet.edu) (see the following page).

Teachers who incorporate rigor are demanding in what they want students to know and are able to do. They provide relevant and engaging lessons. They address different learning styles and provide self-challenging work for the students. Lastly, they are adaptive, able to make changes as student learning progresses or stalls.

Willard R. Daggett, Ed.D., the well-known educator from the International Center for Leadership in Education, has introduced another way to define rigor in the classroom (2012). He suggests that all educators can easily use the Rigor/Relevance Framework to help students become real learners and teachers become more than lecturers.

Another model by consultant and CEO of Essential Learning Services, Randi Trontz, is called the "Recognizing Rigor in the Classroom" (Chart 6.2). According to Trontz:

> Principals and teachers are responsible for identifying rigor in the classroom. Especially with Common Core expectations upon us, rigor takes on a greater role in student achievement for all students. No longer can we provide only Honors or gifted students with the skills and opportunities to meet academic challenges. All students, regardless of age, language, socioeconomics, or parents' education must demonstrate high levels and deep complexity of thought. How will you know if a teacher provides the rigor required of Common Core? Ask the following questions during a classroom walk-through or observation" (2013).

By defining rigor for your teachers, parents, and students, they will have a better understanding of what the end game is all about.

	Words from our "What is Academic Rigor" Acrostic
A	Aligned with standards, **Authentic**, Analysis, Anticipating, Actualizing, Artistic, Across the curriculum
C	**Consistent, collaborative challenging curriculum, Creativity, Complex, Constructivist, Collaborative,**
A	Assessment, Analytic, Adventurous, **Accountable, Authentic assessment, Active learning**
D	Discussion, Develops depth, **Dynamic-diverse thinking, Developmentally appropriate**, Demanding, **Design a dynamic and diverse curriculum**
E	Experiencing educational engagement, Evaluates self, **Energetic engagement, Enriching and engaging**
M	**Motivating, meaningful, multicultural moments, Maximizes multiple intelligences**, Measurable
I	Integrated, **Investigative inquiry**, Individualized, Inquiry-based learning, **Intentional, Inspiring**
C	**Creative and critical thinking, Challenging**, Common Core Standards, **Collaborative**, Concise, Clear, Caring, Creative
R	**Research based**, Responsibility, **Relevant**, Rubric, **Real life**
I	In-depth inquiry, **Instills persistence**, Intentional inquiry, **Intentional formative assessment, Individualized**, Integrated and inclusive curriculum
G	**Going deeper, Grass roots (student choice), Goal oriented**, Grade level expectations, **Growth/goal setting**, Gifted for all
O	Organized and on-going, **On-target for college & career, Opportunities for higher-order thinking, Originality is embraced, Open-ended questioning**, Organic, **Optimizes the use of technology**
R	**Real and relevant, Responsive, Reflective, Rich, Risk-taker, Research-based**

Chart 6.1. What Is Academic Rigor?

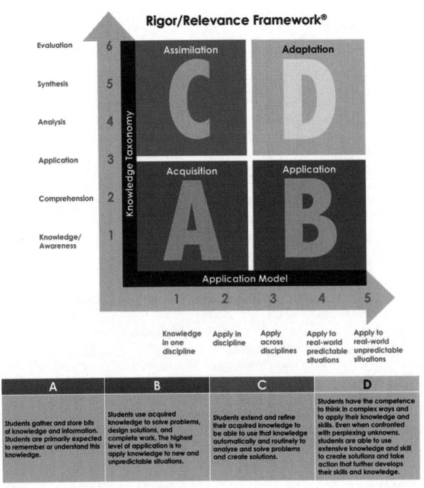

Chart 6.2. Rigor/Relevance Framework

DEMAND RIGOR

It's one thing to have a definition of rigor, it is quite another to demand it of everyone in the district! As a superintendent, you can set the vision, ensure that everyone knows that the vision includes the need for rigor at all levels in all content areas, and then get out of your office to make sure that your vision is in fact a reality in the classrooms and schools for which you are responsible.

As a principal, everything you do should reflect back on the district's vision of a focus on learning and academic rigor. But do you know what you are looking for? Even with a definition of rigor, in order to demand it, you must actualize it. Provide rubrics or detailed information of what you are looking for specifically in the classroom.

For instance, a principal may let the teaching staff know that every walk-through will focus on "the use of project-based learning and other engaging, inquiry-based teaching methods that provide students opportunities to master academic content, learn workforce skills, and develop personal strengths." Now you are demanding rigor in the classroom. Students are not just sitting and listening to lectures or mindlessly answering worksheets. They are think-ing! They are doing! They are engaged! You have demanded rigor.

SUPPORT RIGOR

It is well and good to say we want rigor in the classroom, but what if I am a teacher and I'm not sure what that means? What if I'm a principal and I definitely don't know how to explain it, but I know it when I see it? And what about the students who have not been accustomed to academic rigor? How will they be supported? As a school and district leader, you need to support all of the stakeholders.

Let's take them in reverse order and focus on the students for a moment. According to the Pathways to College Network (2009), "Without strategies to support students in nurturing their talents, building new skills, and master-ing tough challenges, many will be unable to meet these increased academic demands." So we can put into place the greatest programs with the greatest teachers, but without support for students, they are sure to fail.

Students need the support of tutors, learning groups of peers, and extra time with teachers as examples of support. In some states, strong responses to intervention programs are being put in place to ensure students access to a more rigorous curriculum. What are you doing in your district or school for the students?

Support for principals and other site administrators is crucial to a focus on learning and a rigorous academic program. Providing coaches to site admin-istrators is an excellent way to give them support. Much like the students, site administrators also need "tutoring," but with a peer who understands rigor and the unique situation of the school. Coaches are invaluable, as any Olympic athlete will tell you.

In addition to coaching, principals need to have policies and procedures in place in the district that support the demand for rigor. An outgrowth of the policies and procedures should be professional development that assists the administrator in fully understanding what they should be seeing in the classroom. We can no longer assume that good administrators "know"—they don't! The requirements are too many and changing too fast for them all to be proficient in everything. Until you are proven differently, accept the notion that professional development around rigor is necessary, if for nothing else than to define it.

We now can focus on the artists of learning—the teachers. They need support in different ways. They need funding to develop the type of project-based lessons spoken of earlier. They need professional development to know how to begin, and they need time with each other to work on their craft. All of this takes money, time, and thoughtful planning. Do you have it in you to provide the support needed for rigor or are you just giving lip service to it?

A FINAL NOTE

As Nike says, "Just Do It!" Just think about if elite athletes turned their backs on rigor in their training. Pretty soon they would be forgotten!

A recent example was Tiger Woods, who suffered personal, physical, and emotional trauma of his own doing. He quit practicing golf to take care of the above issues, and others with concentration and rigor surpassed him. Rigor was an unthought-of concept prior to Thanksgiving of 2009, when Woods's world came tumbling down. Tiger eventually returned to the rigor of training of his past, but it was catch-up for sure. He's still at the top of the golfing world, but he was very close to a tumble to the bottom. He learned the importance of learning and rigor and has put it back into play.

Therefore, the following six principles focus on learning and academic rigor:

1. Student Learning Is the Chief Responsibility of Everyone
2. Set High Expectations for Learning
3. Collaborate to Determine the Best Thinking
4. Define Rigor
5. Demand Rigor
6. Support Rigor

PRACTICAL SUGGESTIONS

Here are some practical suggestions to focus on learning and academic rigor:

1. Bring everyone in on the action of learning! Include custodians, secretaries, cafeteria workers, and all staff members on the importance of how their jobs interface with the school's job of teaching and learning.

2. Implement an International Baccalaureate Program for Elementary Schools, Middle Schools, and High Schools.
3. Allow all students access to Advanced Placement classes.
4. Provide professional development in project-based and inquiry learning.
5. Develop diagnostic assessments that are flexible enough to meet students' learning needs.
6. Establish nurturing classrooms at all levels.
7. Define rigor for all stakeholders. Make it clear and be sure everyone knows what it means!
8. Have clearly delineated descriptions of what rigor looks like in the classroom.
9. Provide resources for regular collaboration for administrators and teachers.

SOME BOOKS, ARTICLES AND WEBSITES
TO FOCUS ON LEARNING AND ACADEMIC RIGOR

"Academic rigor." Olympic Educational Services District #114 in Bremerton, WA. (www.oesd.wednet.edu).

"A college readiness issue brief: Academic rigor: At the heart of college access and success." Washington DC: Pathways to College Network. 2009.

Daggett, Willard R. *Achieving academic excellence through rigor and relevance.* International Center for Leadership in Education. 2012.

Muller, Robert D. *"Defining rigor in high school: Framework and assessment tool.* Washington D C: National High School Alliance. 2006.

Roueche, Suanne D. (Ed.). *Innovation abstracts.* August 30, 2002: 24 (16).

Savitz-Romer, Mandy, Jole Jager-Hyman, and Ann Coles. "Executive summary: Removing roadblocks to rigor: Linking academic and social supports to ensure college readiness and success." Washington DC: Pathways to College Network. April 2009.

The Hechinger Institute. *Understanding and reporting on academic rigor: A Hechinger Institute primer for journalists.* New York: Teachers College, Columbia University.

Trontz, Randi. "Recognizing rigor in the classroom." 2013.

Chapter Seven

Embedded Professional Development

Rigorous research suggests that sustained and intensive professional learning for teachers is related to student achievement gains. An analysis of well-designed experimental studies found that a set of programs which offered substantial contact hours of professional development (ranging from 30 to 100 hours in total) spread over six to 12 months showed a positive and significant effect on student achievement gains.

—K. S. Yoon

For many years, educators at all levels have been involved in one-day trainings, "make and take it" workshops and lectures on a variety of topics, in order to increase student achievement. Some of these experiences were fairly good, some were just plain awful, and others acted as scattershot—hitting the mark for some teachers who needed or wanted the information and boring others out of their minds! There just had to be a better way to gain new skills and strengthen existing skills than the way education was going about it.

With the onset of site-based management in the late 1980s and 1990s, teachers and staff began to have a say in what "staff development" would be a part of their school plan. Planning days began popping up after a "staff development day" so teachers would have an opportunity to at least talk about what they had learned the previous day or week and how they would implement it in order to help students succeed.

Then around the turn of the 21st century came professional learning communities, giving teachers a designated time to communicate about student achievement and teacher next steps (DuFour, DuFour, Eaker, and Others, 2006). Some principals guided and watched over these meetings to make sure that student achievement issues were in the forefront of all discussion.

At some schools they drifted into additional planning time or grade-level meetings.

It was time to take a look at what was really working! Linda Darling-Hammond, Ruth Chung Wei, Alethea Andree, Nikole Richardson, and Stelios Orphanos—all from the School Redesign Network at Stanford University in Palo Alto, California—did just that with a comprehensive report that was published by the National Staff Development Council in 2009. The following principles are primarily from the study, but additional principles have been included stemming from other research:

PROFESSIONAL DEVELOPMENT SHOULD BE INTENSIVE, ONGOING, AND CONNECTED TO PRACTICE

This principle seems so easy and yet as stated above, it is not something that education has been very good at providing. If we think of the medical field for a moment and the inclusion of interns and resident doctors working in the field with experienced doctors, you realize how far off the mark we have been in providing the intensive, ongoing, and connected-to-practice professional development that has been needed.

Doctors talk about real patients while they are lying in front of them. In private they discuss what the symptoms might mean, what the diagnosis should be, and what the prescription for better health will be. Educators, by contrast, work primarily in isolation at one-shot conferences or professional development sessions. If a teacher really doesn't have the solution to helping students achieve, that solution has no other route of getting into the classroom, unless teachers work together on a regular basis to discuss what in their practice is working to bring up student achievement and what should be discarded. These discussions need to be focused, intense, and regular!

At one school I worked at, a sixth grade student transferred in midyear. He was large for his age and it was soon apparent that he had been retained. The teacher was at a loss as to what to do with him as he sat all day doing absolutely nothing. Luckily, the school believed in and practiced embedded professional development to ensure that all students achieve. Teachers met weekly to discuss their instruction, student achievement, and curriculum. One day, while I was sitting in on one of those meetings, the subject of this young man came up.

As the teachers began discussing his past, his assessments, and his propensity to do nothing, one of the teachers spoke up. He said that his idea might not work, but he thought the teacher should try putting the boy on the computer the next day and see what would happen, not requiring him to do the regular work. This was quite a luxury since the classrooms had few computers to share with an entire class.

The teacher agreed to try it. The next thing the team knew, the boy had typed a 60-page novel. It turned out that he could not write! I was fortunate to see the grin on his face when he received an "A" for his efforts.

The collective minds of that team came up with a solution for a failing boy that turned him into an achieving student. Those teachers provided valuable professional development to each other. They will always remember that solution and try it again when the need arises.

PROFESSIONAL DEVELOPMENT SHOULD FOCUS ON STUDENT LEARNING AND ADDRESS THE TEACHING OF SPECIFIC CURRICULUM CONTENT

Too often we forget about the students when professional development is scheduled. A whole day is often given to how to use the "Teacher's Manual." That in and of itself is not a bad thing, but all too often with shriveling budgets, this may be the only professional development a teacher gets in a year. Or even worse, with no money to purchase new materials, teachers are using outdated materials that are not sufficiently teaching what we now know is best practice.

A successful program focuses on students—their needs, their knowledge, and their learning style in order to reach proficiency. With the data of who each student is, what strengths they possess, and what weakness needs a focus, teachers can then work miracles! But they need time and they need it regularly. They need to be taught how to use the time efficiently and effectively to meet every child's needs.

I have been working in a district that has trained about one-eighth of their teachers to work in professional learning communities, and yet they expect all teachers to be able to use the prescribed time to focus on the students. This is an impossible task for those teachers. They are used to meetings where they discuss field trips, grade level letters, and other important, but unfocused, items. We need to make sure that teachers are trained in how to hold a teacher's meeting that looks at data, discusses student achievement, and can discuss the 21st-century skills. Teachers can't do that if they are not trained.

A high-achieving environment is the result of teachers' knowing how to run a successful meeting about important issues that result in student achievement.

PROFESSIONAL DEVELOPMENT SHOULD ALIGN WITH SCHOOL IMPROVEMENT PRIORITIES AND GOALS

Schools write School Plans for Student Achievement in California, and other states have other names for these plans. The problem is that no one looks at them once they have been approved or until a review process comes along. These plans need to be working, dog-eared documents.

Teachers and staff alike need to be able to rattle off the school priorities and goals and then be able to say without hesitation how those priorities and goals are being met in the classroom with specific students. No excuses! If everyone is in the same boat, paddling up the same river in unison, the endpoint of student proficiency will appear, and it will appear faster and more effectively than any one teacher paddling on their own.

Let's look at the experience of two different schools. One principal I worked with was new to the position, but had been on staff when the plan was conceived and written. The principal had not brought it to the forefront of the staff members' attention all year. When asked about their goals, most stumbled over their words, trying to remember what the previous principal had lead them to develop.

The second school also had a new principal, but this principal had not been on staff prior to taking over the school. Every staff meeting, this principal would have the staff review a part of the school plan. Teachers were well versed in the end game and planned their instruction to be aligned with the agreed upon outcomes.

So which school had the highest jump in student achievement? The answer is too easy. It was the second school, of course! They were all onboard, they were working in unison, and they knew the goal they were all working toward. They also knew that every meeting meant that they were required to discuss how they were working toward the school goals in their classrooms. They named names and spoke with authority about what the students in their rooms needed. Together, they made great strides in student achievement!

PROFESSIONAL DEVELOPMENT SHOULD BUILD STRONG WORKING RELATIONSHIPS AMONG TEACHERS

"Research shows that when schools are strategic in creating time and productive working relationships within academic departments or grade levels, across them, or among teachers school-wide, the benefits can include greater consistency in instruction, more willingness to share practices and try new ways of teaching, and more success in solving problems of practice" (Darling-Hammond, Wei, Andree, Richardson, and Orphanos, 2009).

Education in the 21st century needs all of these benefits to succeed. As education becomes more technology driven, it will become ever more important that some consistency of content and instruction be available to all students to ensure that equity of knowledge and access occurs for all students.

As knowledge explodes around us and students come to us more and more diverse in their culture, language, and background knowledge, teachers will need to be able to share experiences and practices for the good of all. Without strong working relationships, teachers won't want to work together, or if forced, will give it only a cursory attempt at collaboration.

Working simultaneously in two schools that were trying to implement teacher learning communities gave me valuable insight into the process.

In one school, the teachers had strong bonds with each other. As a new member joined each team, the teams drew that teacher in, giving the history of the school, the stories of the staff members, and a piece of themselves in their private life. They built strong personal and working relationships with each other. As a result, their teacher learning communities were constructed on trust and friendship. They were able to freely offer advice about achieving better results and the suggestions were taken in the spirit in which they were given. It was a joy to sit in on their discussions.

In the second school, the teachers were working in their teacher learning communities only when they knew the principal would be stopping by. An unexpected appearance by the principal would find that the team had broken up to do individual projects: running off papers for the entire grade level, getting books out of the library that they would share, or returning to their rooms. The lack of trust among all of the teams was so evident. Academic achievement was not a priority, nor did they even think the students were capable of success. The students mirrored the expectations of the staff.

To give the principal credit that is due, she immediately started looking at the steps of how to turn around that toxic environment and begin building the relationships that would be necessary for her school to exhibit program improvement.

Collaboration that will build the skills necessary for the 21st century are what teachers need to be willing to share and build with each other. Leaders need to plan for time that encourages strong working relationships—not just what the contract allows for, but additional time that will reinforce skills, introduce new concepts, and build on the strengths of the group in each of the individuals on the team. Only then can problems be solved that will move students toward meeting their full potential.

SCHOOL-BASED COACHING
ENHANCES PROFESSIONAL LEARNING

When you think about elite athletes, there is always a coach somewhere close by. Michael Phelps, the great Olympic swimmer, has Bob Bowman. Tiger Woods, who is likely to become the greatest golfer of all times once he passes Jack Nicklaus in Major wins, has had several well-publicized coaches. And who has not heard of Béla Károlyi, the great women's gymnastics coach of Mary Lou Retton? None of these greats could have done it alone. We cheer for them, we put their pictures on Wheaties™ boxes and we read every word we can about them.

Why do we think our teachers need less? Why do we think our teachers can survive, year after year with a beginning-of-the-year pep talk by the superintendent and/or the principal, a few staff development days that they may or may not need, and weekly grade-level meetings? How will our students succeed in such an environment?

To be an elite teacher or administrator is to need a coach. A coach is nonevaluative, but should be honest and direct in assisting the professional educators become more than they currently are. A coach should be a necessity and built into every budget. The results will be well worth the money spent; just ask Michael Phelps.

MENTORING AND INDUCTION PROGRAMS FOR
NEW TEACHERS SUPPORT TEACHER EFFECTIVENESS

In the opening of this chapter, I discussed the process interns and residents go through to become doctors. They have mentors or senior doctors that are by their side as they treat patients. In the television series *House*, interns and residents were involved in some serious conversations and quizzes about patients under their care. Sometimes they were involved in some fairly courageous conversations with House and it didn't always feel good. A mentor who is worth something doesn't just praise the new teacher for trying.

A mentor who is worth something has courageous conversations about what is happening to students in the classrooms. Is the new teacher effective? Why? Why not? What steps does the new teacher need to take to be a more effective teacher who will guide the students to proficiency and beyond? Mentors and induction programs have been shown to be the best investment in new teachers (Strong, 2005).

Money is scarce, but those new teachers will become tenured and have an effect on thousands of students over their career. Wouldn't it be better if it were a positive effect?

PROFESSIONAL DEVELOPMENT SHOULD STEM FROM TEACHER SELF-ASSESSED NEEDS, EVALUATION NEEDS, AND STUDENT ACHIEVEMENT NEEDS

Oftentimes superintendents, board members, principals, and, yes, even members of Congress hear about the latest and greatest to cure the ills of the schools in their district. They rush back to the district and immediately, by fiat, implement the program. There is no buy in. There is no understanding of the context of which the program was sold. Teachers only know it is theirs to implement and achieve higher test scores, better results!

But what does research tell us? In adult learning theory, if teachers are a part of the problem solving, they will be a part of the solution and do so eagerly (Nevills 2011). Districts that assess teacher needs and then plan for appropriate, embedded professional development over extended periods will find that teachers become more excited about implementation, they master the program more quickly, and the students achieve at a higher level because the teachers really believe in what they are doing.

According to Nevills, "Adults have three distinguishing behavioral characteristics as learners:

1. Adults learn most effectively when they have input into what they will be learning.
2. Mature learners want to apply what they are learning to what they currently need in their personal, career, or professional lives.
3. Active engagement with learning results from internal motivation and not through prompting. (Nevills, 2011)

If professional development is planned based on these three characteristics, then teachers will be actively engaged in ensuring that the best instructional practices and 21st-century skills are being offered to their students. It will happen because they are given enough interesting information about research-based practices that they will be curious to learn more and will ask for further information.

But it is the leader's job to make sure that teachers are aware of what professional development is available and then let them self-assess their needs, keeping in mind the final prize—that student achievement and success must be the end result!

TECHNOLOGY IS A NECESSARY FOCUS OF ALL PROFESSIONAL DEVELOPMENT

Have you watched a 2-year-old with a tablet or a smartphone? These youngsters are intuitive with technology. They only get frustrated when the battery dies. Everything else they seem to figure out without your help. They know their favorite apps, the sounds each makes, and the characters who bounce around their screens. We then send them to school and if they are really lucky, they may get to touch technology for 20 to 45 minutes a day.

Some districts are going to the other extreme and spending fortunes on tablets without a real plan for how to use them. Professional development must teach the teachers how to incorporate technology as easily as a pencil. Technology should be a part of an English language arts training as much as a science training.

As we move forward into the 21st century, the students with the technology skills will become the achievers. Some states are even administering achievement tests online. What happens to the students whose teacher isn't confident enough to use technology when it's time to take the test? Is it a knowledge and application issue, or is it a failure to understand the technology due to lack of practice? It's time to ensure that professional development does not occur without the inclusion of some sort of technology. Your students will thank you!

REFLECTION IS A BEST PRACTICE FOR ALL

How many times have you said to yourself, "I just wish I had time to think!"? Reflection allows us thinking time. Embedded professional development gives teachers that gift that they have been asking for: time to think.

Take a minute and think about a time you had a problem to solve or something you wanted to learn. I can almost guarantee you that you wanted some alone time to think about it or practice what you had just learned. Many times when I am facing a problem I find my reflective time just before I go to sleep. I think about the problem, asking myself questions. Then as I sleep, my brain takes over as I quiet down. More times than not, I will have a solution or the beginning of an idea for implementation when I wake up. Our brains need us to slow down so they can think, even if our bodies don't want to (Cashman, 2012).

So as leaders and administrators we need to provide our teachers and our students—and don't forget yourself—the reflective time needed to learn, to remember, and to solve problems.

According to Ghaye (2011), reflective practice should center around these four questions:

1. What's working well?
2. What needs changing?
3. What are we learning?
4. Where do we go from here?

Ending each session with an action plan that reflects on the answers to these questions, the practice that makes teachers think about what is going well because students are achieving, and what isn't going well because students just didn't get it, gives teachers time to reflect on their practice. Reflection leads to honing their skills and becoming experts at what they do. Give them that gift and practice reflection yourself. You will be pleased with the results in teacher instruction and student achievement.

A FINAL NOTE

Professional development needs to be integrated into the whole. What are the initiatives already in place at the school? How does this new one fit? Is it on top of, or integrated into? Teachers will have stronger buy in if it is integrated into a thoughtful plan and if it meets their needs! Remember adult learning theory if you want successful embedded professional development.

These are the eight principles related to embedded professional development:

1. Professional development should be intensive, ongoing and connected to practice.
2. Professional development should align with school improvement priorities and goals.
3. Professional development should build strong working relationships among teachers.
4. School-based coaching enhances professional learning.
5. Mentoring and induction programs for new teachers support teacher effectiveness.

6. Professional development should stem from teacher self-assessed needs, evaluation needs, and student achievement needs.
7. Technology is a necessary focus of all professional development.
8. Reflection is a best practice for all.

PRACTICAL SUGGESTIONS

Here are some practical suggestions for embedded professional development.

1. Survey teachers as to what they need and to what degree they need additional instruction.
2. Include in professional development application of the knowledge being learned, right there, on the spot.
3. Stress a topic for professional development that should be continuous over months and years to ensure implementation.
4. There should be a regular and consistent way to monitor the implementation of new learning by teachers.
5. Provide them opportunities for hands-on work as the teachers are learning the content.
6. Define clearly how students will flourish and learn if the strategy being introduced is implemented. What is the end game?
7. Include data assessment in professional development. How does the current strategy increase the possibility of success?
8. Provide ongoing support for any new implementation if you want it to work! This is where a coach or a mentor becomes so important.
9. Build in professional learning communities, teacher learning communities, or student focus groups, or whatever strong, interactive professional teams to discuss instructional strategies, formative and summative assessment, and curriculum and student progress. Give your teachers time and direction to accomplish what is needed to become a high performing team.
10. Allow teachers to observe each other and provide feedback.
11. Include technology in all professional development.
12. Include mentors for new teachers and coaches for experienced teachers as a part of the school/district culture.
13. Institutionalize reflection and reflective practice through the use of the four questions, an action plan, or individual logs.

SAMPLE CHART FOR ASSESSING PROFESSIONAL DEVELOPMENT

Criteria for Effective Professional Development

For each criterion, mark the appropriate rubric number for the degree of implementation.

Criteria	Professional Development Name			
	No	A Few	Most	All
1. Teachers were surveyed for need.	1	2	3	4
2. Integrated into other Initiatives	1	2	3	4
3. Application of the knowledge being learned, right there, on the spot.	1	2	3	4
4. Topic embedded and continuous	1	2	3	4
5. Monitoring of new learning	1	2	3	4
6. Teachers learn in context	1	2	3	4
7. Define how students will achieve	1	2	3	4
8. Includes assessment data	1	2	3	4
9. Provides ongoing support	1	2	3	4
10. Direction for high-performing team	1	2	3	4
11. Teachers observe each other	1	2	3	4
12. Technology is included	1	2	3	4
13. Mentors and coaches provided	1	2	3	4
14. Reflection occurs often	1	2	3	4
	1	2	3	4
	1	2	3	4

Chart 7.1.   Criteria For Effective Professional Development

1. What's working well?

_____

_____

_____

_____

2. What needs changing?

_____

_____

_____

_____

3. What are we learning?

_____

_____

_____

_____

4. Where do we go from here?

_____

_____

_____

_____

Chart 7.2.   Reflection Log

SOME BOOKS, ARTICLES, AND WEBSITES
TO IMPLEMENT EMBEDDED
PROFESSIONAL DEVELOPMENT

Cashman, Kevin. *The pause principle*. San Francisco: Berrett-Koehler. 2012.

Darling-Hammond, Linda, Ruth Chung Wei, Alethea Andree, Nikole Richardson, and Stelios Orphanos. *Profession learning in the learning profession: A status report on teacher development in the United States and abroad.* Stanford, CA: National Staff Development Council, Stanford University. 2009.

DuFour, R. P., and Others. *Learning by doing: A handbook for professional learning communities at work.* Bloomington, IN: Solution Tree. 2006.

Ghaye, Tony. *Teaching and learning through reflective practice: A practical guide for positive action.* Taylor & Francis. 2011.

Nevills, Pamela, *Build the brain for reading: Grades 4–12*. Corwin Press. 2011.

Professional learning communities. http://books.google.com/books?hl=en&lr=&id=J-TETSs7P6EC&oi=fnd&pg=PA1&dq=embedded+professional+development+education&ots=Q96rIqqBRZ&sig=WARmXshVn-vSVKv4eXFX1a087N4#v=onepage&q=embedded%20professional%20development%20education&f=false.

Strong, Michael. *Mentoring new teachers to increase retention: A look at the research.* Santa Cruz: New Teacher Center, University of California Santa Cruz. 2005.Yoon, K. S. and Others. "Reviewing the evidence on how teacher professional development affects student achievement." *Issues & Answers Report.* REL 2007: No. 03. Washington D.C. U.S. Department of Education, Institute of Education Sciences, National Center for Education Evaluation and Regional Assistance, Regional Education Laboratory Southwest. Retrieved from http://ies.ed.gov/ncee/edlabs/regions/southwest/pdf/REL_2007033pdf and http://64.78.6.92/library/schoolbasedlitreview.pdf.

Chapter Eight

Academic Achievement and Assessment for the 21st Century

> I am calling on our nation's governors and state education chiefs to develop standards and assessments that don't simply measure whether students can fill in a bubble on a test, but whether they possess 21st Century Skills like problem solving and critical thinking, entrepreneurship and creativity.

> —President Barack Obama

President Obama is asking a lot of the educational community, our politicians, and our state educational leaders, but a lot is needed to prepare our youth for the future they have ahead of them. If we think of the changes that have occurred just since Apple gave every school one computer back in the early 1980s, it is truly amazing. We didn't know we needed that technology and now we can't live without it. Take away the technology of most people for even a day and they will scream for it back.

So as we look at education in the 21st century, should assessment and evaluation look like pre-1980s? Isn't it time that we begin to look at what academic achievement we want our students to really have and be able to do and then design assessments that truly test those skills? Without such assessments, we are dooming our students to a life stuck in the 20th century.

Now that wouldn't be so bad for you and me—that's when we grew up, but think of the children of today who have never been without technology. Think about the two-year-old who can grab a tablet or a smartphone and know how to use it. And yet we are still giving 21st-century students 20th-century multiple-choice tests that test little of what they are going to need to know in their future.

Throughout the country, schools do not even have enough computers to administer the soon to be developed Common Core Standards test (Meador,

2012)! So while the test is being written, the technology is not in place to administer it and the students do not have the skills necessary to take the assessment. Something is wrong with this picture and we need to adjust the focus!

The principles that follow aim to do just that, to begin the conversation about matching what we want for our 21st-century students to how we will know that they know it.

ASSESSMENT MUST RESPOND TO 21ST CENTURY SKILLS

Looking at a current summative assessment, one would not be able to tell if it was 1950, 1980, or 2012 because the skills being assessed are similar in nature. Visually, not much has changed except for updated stories and pictures.

Certainly 21st-century tests such as the California Star Test (CST) or the Iowa Test of Basic Skills (ITBS) are trying to provide increased numbers of higher-level questions in the test than previous years and for that they are given credit.

However, are they really including all the skills necessary to navigate the 21st century efficiently? While different sources use a variation on the theme, the skills presented below are the ones most commonly mentioned as the 21st Century Skills:

- Collaboration
- Cooperation
- Communication
- Creativity
- Organization and research
- Problem solving
- Self-direction/social responsibility
- Technology skills

(Wagner, 2008; Harvey, 2011)

But schools and students are still being evaluated on multiple-choice tests that may be computer based, so there is a nod to technology skills, and have a fair amount of problem solving in the questions, but they are still multiple choice! And there is a place for multiple-choice tests—just not to assess 21st Century Skills. Multiple- choice tests are quick and give us information about students' academic achievement in basic skills such as computing and reading comprehension. They should not be discarded, but retooled for their uses.

There is a huge disconnect between what we want from our students in skill development and what we assess them in for achievement and college readiness. Most universities and colleges look at the SAT and ACT scores combined with grades for admission. What does that tell the university or college about a student's ability to collaborate, cooperate, communicate, be creative, show organizational and research skills, solve problems, be self-directed or socially responsible, and finally, have achieved mastery of technology skills?

Unless a high school teacher has graded on these competencies, it tells the universities and colleges only one thing: the student has mastered the skill of multiple-choice test taking—not a 21st-century skill! It is time to make changes in the way we assess students in the classroom, at the end of units, at the end of courses, and at the end of years!

Performance assessment has been around for quite a while and in various stages of use. It is only through watching students collaborate on a real-life problem or be given time for in-depth research to use critical thinking to solve a dilemma, that we really know what students are able to do. Assessments for the 21st century need to be open ended as they are in the highest achieving nations. "These nations use primarily open-ended assessments that call for extensive writing, research, and applications of knowledge to novel situations" (Darling-Hammond, and Adamson 2010).

As we move forward with Common Core Standards and 21st Century Skills, it is imperative that we change the way we assess and evaluate the academic achievement of our students: implementing much more performance assessment, relegating multiple-choice tests to the level at which they are best used—for trend data, and ensuring that all teachers are highly proficient in the use of formative assessment.

FORMATIVE ASSESSMENT IS MORE INTEGRAL TO STUDENTS' SUCCESS THAN SUMMATIVE ASSESSMENTS

So, our second principle turns to formative assessment or assessment *for* learning rather than the aforementioned summative assessments that are assessments *of* learning. Above, as we spoke of multiple-choice tests and in most cases performance assessments, we were talking about what a student has learned about a subject, hence assessment *of* their learning, before moving on to a new subject.

Assessment *for* learning asks the teacher to know minute-by-minute and day-by-day where every student in the class is in their learning, so there is still time to reteach. The learning for the subject or concept is not over. In order for teachers to know what students know at any given time of the period or day, a plethora of techniques must be learned. There are many models of formative assessment to look into.

Educational Testing Service (ETS) developed a program called *Keeping Learning on Track™ (KLT™)*, and the program is now owned by Northwest Evaluation Association (NWEA). This program is a robust professional development program based on the research of Paul Black and Dylan Wiliam (1998). Black and Wiliam are considered the "Fathers of Formative Assessment" and almost every reference returns the reader back to their seminal work, "Inside the Black Box."

Formative Assessment, though, gives teachers a myriad of tools for checking on student learning. With *KLT™*, teachers and students gather evidence of learning and adapt classroom behavior to meet immediate learning needs to accelerate student growth.

Rick Stiggins, Judith Arter, Stephen Chappuis, and Jan Chappuis have continued to develop the concept of formative assessment as they work with teachers in assessment *for* learning. They are very clear in the definitions and applications of what formative assessment should look like. For instance, "when teachers assess student learning for purely formative purposes, there is no final mark on the paper and no summative grade in the grade book. Rather, assessment serves as practice for students, just like a meaningful homework assignment does. This is formative assessment at its most valuable. Called assessment *for* learning, it supports learning in two ways:

- Teachers can adapt instruction on the basis of evidence, making changes and improvements that will yield immediate benefits to student learning.
- Students can use evidence of their current progress to actively manage and adjust their own learning. (Stiggins, Arter, Chappuis, and Chappuis, 2006)

Caroline Wylie (2010) from ETS has developed a webinar that shows how formative assessment can be used in the classroom using diagnostic questions. The use of diagnostic questions during lessons has a huge impact on student learning in mathematics and science, but the formative assessment technique can definitely be used in all content areas. She has developed a webinar where she explains how the use of diagnostic questions fits within the larger framework of formative assessment; she describes the research project she carried out and the resulting outcomes.

Dr. Wylie, who worked with Dylan Wiliam, illustrates how teachers used these questions in the classroom to identify and address students' mathematical and scientific misconceptions. Once a teacher can identify the misconceptions of students learning, it is much easier to teach the accurate information. Diagnostic questions open the door to identifying misconceptions and to learning.

These are but three resources that an administrator can turn to in order to provide professional development for teachers. There are many more. The caveat is to make sure that the training for formative assessment or assessment for learning is embedded and that the techniques are used consistently by every teacher on the staff. No excuses!

One school that implemented a focused formative assessment process found that the students became so used to knowing what each lesson's learning intention was, that if a teacher did not have it posted and refer to it, the students asked "What are we learning today?" and "How will you know if we learned it?" (success criteria).

The students knew that teachers were going to be asking a lot of diagnostic questions throughout the lessons and that everyone would be held responsible for answering the questions. They also knew that this was learning time, not testing time, so they trusted the process, asking questions, admitting when they didn't know the answer, and listening carefully when someone else did. When you see a totally engaged classroom, where learning is very apparent, it is indeed a sight to behold! Formative assessment practices allow for a learning classroom!

USE MULTIPLE ASSESSMENTS

No one assessment can give you all of the answers and yet districts, schools, and students are being judged on one standardized test! Just think if you were promoted or even paid on the outcome of just one task you were asked to perform. You would think it outrageous and yet that is what we do to our students and soon, in many states, to our teachers.

It is important to judge students, teachers, administrators, and schools on multiple types of assessments. In the era of accountability, this is even more important. School districts have incorporated benchmark assessments and that is great. However, most benchmark assessments are summative. There isn't time to go back and reteach once a benchmark test is given. The pacing guides in place move the teacher and students forward, ready or not!

That is why multiple assessments between benchmark assessments are critical for learning. Given at smaller incremental steps along the learning path, students and teachers have time to reteach, comprehend, and become confident learners. Only with multiple assessments can the true picture of a student's knowledge emerge.

USE DATA OVER AND OVER AGAIN

Data are plural, which means we need to keep coming back to them. I am working with a district that is very high achieving. They get their scores in the fall, see that they remain high, congratulate themselves, and move on.

What they didn't notice was that one of their subgroups had continually lost ground. It was lost in the overall high scores they were achieving. It was time to change the way they were looking at data. A specialist was brought in to show them how to read the myriad of reports that came with the "high scores." Without prompting, when shown the right reports, they began to see the downward patterns.

It is important to really dig into that data throughout the year. Take time at faculty meetings or principal meetings to look more carefully at one small piece of the data each meeting. The same is true for benchmark assessments, Friday spelling tests, end of chapter mathematics tests, and so on. Each time you look at data, you will find something new or surprising, and you will be asking yourself, "Why haven't I noticed that before?" It's because you weren't looking! Looking at data should be routine. Make decisions about program, personnel, and budget only after perusing the appropriate data in depth.

USE DATA ASSIDUOUSLY TO IMPROVE

So, now that you are looking at the data more often, what are you seeing? The district mentioned above noticed their English Language Learners (ELLs) really weren't doing so well. Okay, now what?

They brought in an ELL specialist who trained the principals in what good lessons looked like for ELL students. The principals and teachers then learned the instructional strategies that work for ELL students and decided on three that they would teach and require all teachers to use. The district administrators and the principals did walk-throughs of designated classrooms with an agreed upon rubric in hand. After each classroom visit they stopped and discussed what they saw. They used the test data and the observation data to improve instruction.

This year when their test scores arrived, they did not stop with the overall numbers, they went immediately to the subgroup of ELL students. After just one year of focus, every school's ELL population had higher scores, stopping a downward trend. They took their data seriously and used it assiduously to improve!

YOU MUST USE TREND DATA

Looking at data has been in vogue for many years now. Teachers and school administrators are asked to analyze the data that is returned from benchmark and annual state testing. The problem arises when those educators aren't really trained in how to look at data. They may be able to see changes from year to year, but is there dedicated time to look beyond the obvious?

As mentioned above, especially high-scoring schools and districts sometimes fail to look closely at the trend data. Another district had bragging rights to their high scores, but never noticed a slow downward trend in mathematics was occurring. Again, because the overall scores remained fairly high they didn't go deeper. In some cases it was one grade level that was pulling up the overall mathematics scores.

When we started looking at the trend data, the principals were aghast! How had this happened and they never noticed? It was due to reliance on overall scores and looking at just two years in a row. To really see trends it is recommended that administrators and teachers look at four or five years of data. That's where the real story lies.

With today's technology it should be easy, but we are finding that other "stuff" gets in the way of really drilling down into the data. It is important that it becomes a district priority and that time is set aside at all level of meetings to look at it carefully. The motto for every district and school should be: "Analyze, Discuss, Act!"

IT TAKES A TEAM TO ANALYZE DATA

In order to "Analyze, Discuss, and Act," teachers and administrators must be working in teams or there won't be any discussion. A team allows you to look at the data in different ways, look at the reasons for the scores from different vantage points, and be able to come up with a variety of actions to take to move toward higher achievement.

It is the principal's responsibility to ensure that meetings happen and they do in fact focus on data, if that is the reason for the meeting. Oftentimes, it is easy to digress into lesson planning once one area of deficit is discovered. The team must have persistence to stay at it. They will find that one discovery leads to another and the picture becomes much bigger than one concept or a different lesson plan.

Give them time, but give them the skills to analyze data together. It is still amazing to me that we are giving presentations on how to read and interpret data. This should be a core skill of every educator. Do all of your teachers and administrators have the core skill to work in a productive team to analyze, discuss, and act?

COMMON CORE STANDARDS
ARE CHANGING ASSESSMENT

The Common Core Standards are coming to most states by 2014. Are you ready for the changes that are going to occur in assessment as a result? Here is an example of a classroom lesson in mathematics for fourth grade that is being recommended by the P21 Partnership (http://www.p21.org/storage/documents/P21CommonCoreToolkit.pdf):

Sample Student Outcome: Students use math content knowledge to understand basic concepts of financial literacy.

Students compare and contrast the same balance in different types of bank accounts to determine which is better for what circumstances (e.g., is a savings account better than a checking account?). Students determine the difference that interest rates make in each account (compound vs. simple interest), compare short and long term costs of borrowing money. Students use mathematical arguments to answer classic questions like, "Which is more: one million dollars, or one penny the first day, double that penny the next day, then double the previous day's pennies and so on for a month?"

A Sample Assessment: Students are asked to develop a plan for their own savings account. They must end up with $3,000 in two years. They cannot deposit all of the money at one time. How much per week would be set aside, why? In what type of account? Show how it is compounded.

Or in English Language Arts for 8th grade, the teacher may plan something like this, according to the P21 Partnership:

Sample Student Outcome: Analyze, compare and contrast authors' and artists' motivations for creativity.

EXAMPLE: In this unit, students step back and consider the motivations of authors and artists alike: What inspires artists? How is it similar and different from that which inspires authors? How is the process of creating a painting or sculpture similar to and different from the process of writing a story or poem? Students also read books written about artists, and study art that can be seen in museums across America. Students work with classmates to uncover the unspoken meanings behind words and artwork. In addition to fine art, students discuss illustrations and other forms of commercial art, looking for similarities to and differences from fine art, both in motivation and presentation styles. They write an informative/explanatory piece about an artist of interest.

A Sample Assessment: This unit ends with an open-ended reflective essay response to the essential question.

The Common Core Standards are rigorous and for all students. They will be the following:

1. Aligned with college and work expectations
2. Focused and coherent
3. Composed of rigorous content and application of knowledge through high-order skills
4. Built upon strengths and lessons of current state standards
5. Internationally benchmarked so that all students are prepared to succeed in our global economy and society
6. Based on evidence and research

We are in different times with different expectations. The Common Core Standards will help every student rise to his or her potential.

USE CRITERIA THAT ARE AUTHENTIC

In each of the same assessments for the Common Core Standards, the assessments aligned with the lessons and the criteria for grading were authentic, meaning that they are based on what the student is actually asked to learn and do. In order for criteria to be authentic teachers must learn to work backwards.

- What is it I want students to know and be able to do?
- How will I know that they know?
- What questions or tasks will I give them in order to know?
- What lesson should I plan that will lead them directly to what I want them to know and be able to do?

If these questions are asked continuously during planning, then the criteria for grading will be authentic and fair. The students will be led in a natural progression to the knowledge required in the Common Core Standards and to the skills of the 21st century.

A FINAL NOTE

Assessment is necessary. Data are the result. Both the assessment and the analysis of the data must focus on higher achievement for all students. Students expect to achieve and with the 21st Century Skills and Common Core Standards arriving on every classroom's doorstep, it is the duty of the adults to be sure that the incoming kindergartner's excitement for learning is the same as the outgoing senior's in high school. You must teach with your heart and evaluate with your brain. The principles in this chapter will make that happen when you adhere to them.

Therefore, the following nine principles lead to Academic Achievement and Assessment for the 21st century:

- Assessment must respond to 21st Century Skills.
- Formative assessment is more integral to students' success than summative assessments.
- Use multiple assessments.
- Use data over and over again.
- Use data assiduously to improve.
- You must use trend data.
- It takes a team to analyze data.
- Common Core Standards are changing assessment.
- Use criteria that are authentic.

PRACTICAL SUGGESTIONS

Here are some practical suggestions for Academic Achievement and Assessment for the 21st century:

1. Identify the 21st Century Skills you want your students to master.
2. Determine the performance assessments to be used to determine mastery of the 21st Century Skills.
3. Develop a consistent grading system that incorporates both the 21st Century Skills and the Common Core Standards in order for teachers, parents, students and the community to know what the grades really mean.
4. Provide all teachers professional development in the use of formative assessment or assessment *for* learning.
5. Provide ongoing, embedded professional development in analyzing assessment data, so trends can be recognized.

SOME BOOKS, ARTICLES, AND WEBSITES TO SUPPORT ACADEMIC ACHIEVEMENT AND ASSESSMENT FOR THE 21ST CENTURY

Black, P., C. Harrison, C. Lee, B. Marshall, and D. Wiliam. "Working inside the black box: Assessment for learning in the classroom." *Phi Delta Kappan.* 2004: 86(1), pp. 9–21.

Black, P., and D. Wiliam. "Inside the black box, raising standards through classroom assessment." *Phi Delta Kappan.* October 1998: 80, pp. 139–148.

Black, P., and D. Wiliam. "Developing the theory of formative assessment." *Educational Assessment, Evaluation, and Accountability.* 2009: 21(1), pp. 5–31. doi: 10.1007/s11092-008-9068-5.

Chappuis, Jan, Rick J. Stiggins, Steve Chappuis, Judith A. Arter. *Classroom assessment for student learning: Doing it right—Using it well* (2nd ed.). Pearson. 2011.

Darling-Hammond, Linda, and Frank Adamson. *Beyond basic skill: The role of performance assessment in achieving 21st century standards of learning.* Stanford Center for Opportunity Policy in Education (SCOPE), Stanford University, School of Education. Retrieved from http://edpolicy.stanford.edu.

Education Connection's Center for 21st Century Skills. 355 Goshen Road, PO Box 909, Litchfield, CT 06759, 860.567.0863, Fax: 860.567.3381. Retrieved from http://www.skills21.org/.

Formative Assessments, STEM, http://www.stemresources.com/index.php?option= com_content&view=article&id=52&Itemid=70.

Harvey, Thomas. *21st century schools.* La Verne, CA: EPIC Monograph. 2011.

Meador, Derrick. "Common Core Assessment: An overview of the Common Core Standards Assessment." 2012. Retrieved from http://teaching.about.com/od/assess/a/Common-Core-Assessment.htm.

P21 toolkit; A guide to aligning the Common Core State Standards with the Framework for 21st Century Skills. Retrieved from http://www.p21.org/storage/documents/P21CommonCoreToolkit.pdf.

Stiggins, R., J. Arter, J. Chappius, and S. Chappius. *Classroom assessment for student learning: Doing it right, using it well.* Assessment Training Institute. 2006.

Wylie, Caroline. "Part II: Formative and diagnostic assessment approaches in math & science." TeachersSERVCenter, University of North Carolina at Greensboro. March 22, 2010. Retrieved from http://www.serve.org/assessment-webinar.aspx.

Chapter Nine

The Strength of Teams

> Never doubt that a small group of thoughtful, committed, citizens can change the world. Indeed, it is the only thing that ever has.
>
> —Margaret Mead

The well-known quote by Margaret Mead was purposively selected to introduce this chapter on the strength of teams for supporting the vision of high student achievement. Great leaders and achievers in our history have recognized the importance of the support of others to accomplish great things.

It has been purported over the years that the great inventor Thomas Edison was once asked why he had a team of twenty-one assistants and his response was, "If I could solve all the problems myself, I would." Well, if you or I could solve all the problems and come up with all the best working strategies for promoting successful student achievement, we would do so in a heartbeat.

The reality is no one person can accomplish this at a school site, a district, or at the state level (Grubb and Flessa, 2006). It does take a team of dedicated people with a common vision for high student achievement as evidenced by the many studies involving schools and districts that are using the collaborative team concept to raise student achievement (Ulrich, 1996; Wiseman, 2010).

The following five team principles support the strong leader's vision to develop successful, high-functioning teams with a focus on and action toward increasing student achievement.

HIGH-ACHIEVEMENT ENVIRONMENTS CANNOT EXIST WITHOUT HIGH-FUNCTIONING TEAMS

There is a wealth of literature on the subject of building and sustaining high-functioning teams (Harvey and Drolet, 2006; Katzenbach and Smith, 1993; Lencioni, 2002). This literature on teams spans a variety of organizational environments but supports a common theme that suggests that no matter what the environment, teams do have a measurable impact on performance if done right (Katzenbach and Smith, 2003).

There are also a number of studies conducted and books written in the past 10 years on the importance of establishing a collaborative culture as an important step toward increasing student achievement (DuFour and Others, 2006; Feger and Arruda, 2008; Kruse, Louis, & Bryk, 1994).

The movement toward establishing Professional Learning Communities (PLC) is an action taken by many schools and districts to support higher student achievement. Hord (1997) indicates that a PLC is an infrastructure or a way of working together that results in continuous school improvement. Reichstetter's (2006) work establishes that an important part of increasing student achievement is when team members regularly collaborate about continued improvement in meeting learner needs.

The research in the past builds a strong case for the importance of collaboration among stakeholders who have the ability to impact student achievement if there is going to be a significant and sustainable increase over time. Recent studies have provided strong evidence to indicate the importance of high-functioning teams as a key component in establishing the collaborative culture for PLCs and non-PLCs to promote and sustain greater student achievement (Buenrostro, 2012; Simon, 2012; Wiseman, 2008).

It is the preponderance of evidence that collaborative teams are key to supporting higher student achievement that emboldens us to declare: High-achievement environments cannot exist without high-functioning teams.

EVERYBODY MUST ROW IN THE SAME DIRECTION

This principle brings to mind a great memory from the past. My wife and I were on a cruise with our dear friends from childhood and we went on a shore excursion in Cancun for snorkeling and kayaking in a gorgeous bay. My wife and I hopped in our kayak and started to paddle out into the bay. We were not experienced and we immediately found that we were not making good headway. At that point we discussed the need to coordinate our efforts while paddling.

It was clear that if we were not rowing together in the same direction we would actually be fighting each other's efforts and would not arrive at the intended reef for good snorkeling. Once we established this common purpose, we immediately rowed off to our intended spot.

The starting point for all teams is to establish a strong sense of purpose or direction. Hill and Lineback (2011) wrote on this very thing for the *Harvard Business Review* in their article titled "The Fundamental Purpose of Your Team." They state, "A clear and compelling purpose is the glue that binds together a group of individuals. It is the foundation on which the collective 'we' of a real team is built" (Hill and Lineback, 2011, para. 10). They emphasize that the leader needs to establish this purpose with the team or the team may never come together to work as a collective whole to accomplish their intended purpose, such as increasing student achievement.

The principle "everyone must row in the same direction" to improve student achievement should be no surprise given the literature on effective teams. There are many different definitions of "team," however most of the accepted definitions proclaim the importance of the common purpose or everyone rowing in the same direction. This purpose or direction for all teams at the school site and/or district should reflect the vision for supporting higher student achievement.

Research has established that people in an organization or members of a team want to believe they are doing something that is important and are making a positive difference for others (O'Reilly and Pfeffer, 2000). A strong common purpose can serve to bring the team members together in pursuit of a larger quest, one that is larger than the individuals on the team and supports team members' buy-in (Mealiea and Baltazar, 2005).

Hopefully, everyone reading this book has had an experience where they felt they were part of a team that was acting to accomplish a very worthy purpose. When you are on a team with this strong purpose, you find that each step forward, small or large, toward that purpose serves as a motivator for all to try harder and do more to achieve the goal. Katzenbach (2003) wrote a book titled *Why Pride Matters More than Money* in which he establishes a strong argument that a sense of purpose, as well as pride, are the most powerful motivating forces in the world and that it is the role of the leader to establish this strong feeling of common purpose for the members of their organization.

The importance of the leader establishing this clear sense of purpose to get team member buy-in and have them all striving to row in the same direction can be illustrated by Coach Phil Jackson's description in his book titled *Sacred Hoops: Spiritual Lessons of a Hardwood Warrior* (1995) regarding the time he coached the Chicago Bulls to six NBA titles, including the famous "three-peat." Jackson talks about his efforts to establish a strong sense of purpose in each player and to constantly remind them of the goal in sight and that they were part of a meaningful quest. He explains the importance of this common purpose when he writes:

> The most effective way to forge a winning team is to call on the players' need to connect to something larger than themselves. Even for those who don't consider themselves "spiritual" in a conventional sense, creating a successful team—whether it's an NBA champion or a record-setting sales force—is essentially a spiritual act. It requires the individuals involved to surrender their self-interest for the greater good so that the whole adds up to more than the sum of its parts (Jackson and Delehanty, 1995).

Educational leaders who are dedicated to improving student achievement can take this lesson from Coach Jackson and apply it to their leadership. Like Coach Jackson, educational leaders should establish teams with a strong sense of purpose for improving student achievement. This strong sense of purpose will empower the team members to connect to a meaningful quest and serve to coordinate their efforts so they are rowing in the same direction!

EVERYBODY HAS A ROLE IN HIGH ACHIEVEMENT

Who should participate in encouraging high expectations? Everybody! When it comes to developing teams at the site and/or district that are focused on student achievement, the leader should include what the literature discusses as the collective leadership (Firestone and Martinez, 2007; Harris and Lambert, 2003; Hiller, Day, and Vance, 2006).

Leithwood and Mascall (2008), from the Ontario Institute for Studies in Education at the University of Toronto, conducted a study to inquire about the different sources of collective leadership for higher achieving schools. They concluded, "Higher-achieving schools awarded leadership influence to all school members and other stakeholders to a greater degree than that of lower-achieving schools. These differences were most significant in relation to the leadership exercised by school teams, parents, and students" (p. 529).

The literature is clear that everybody does have a role in supporting high student achievement (DuFour and DuFour, 2011; Firestone and Martinez, 2007; Harris and Lambert, 2003; Hiller, Day, and Vance, 2006; Hord, 1997). The key for a leader is to thoughtfully craft teams at the site and district that reflect the collective leadership. Site teams should reflect a balance of members including teachers, parents, administrators, and students. Site grade level teams or department teams may reflect teachers only. District teams focused on student achievement should include parents, teachers, community, administrators, and students if applicable.

Establishing teams with collective leaders is important for impacting student achievement. Successful teams also need to have a balance of roles so members will feel motivated and believe they are making a significant difference (Hill and Lineback, 2011). I recall my first year as a principal. I was assigned a K–6 elementary school that had a history of infighting and toxic relations with the former principal and the PTA leadership. When I started asking folks about how they got things done at the school, it became very apparent that the former leader had relied on the same two to three people to counsel with and make all the decisions.

This complete lack of balance of participation had produced a climate of mistrust where teachers were feeling devalued and removed from any of the important initiatives and decisions regarding student achievement. They perceived no valuable connection with the PTA leadership/organization. I started asking a variety of teachers to serve on important decision-making teams and encouraged them to contribute. I also started including parents and PTA parent leaders on the same teams.

I remember one particular teacher telling me she did not think she should be a part of the school leadership team because she did not have much to contribute. For years she had not been asked to participate and she honestly believed she would not be value-added. Well, as you might guess, by the end of the first year she was one of the most enthusiastic members of the leadership team and was respected by all for her contribution.

Too often organizations tend to select the same few "go to" people who leadership perceives to be the doers they can depend upon to get the job accomplished. This tunnel vision of team selection can impact a site or district's success in seeking high achievement for all students.

Research on high-achieving schools supports the need for balanced roles on collaborative teams (Leithwood and Mascall, 2008; Wiseman, 2008). As pointed out by Drolet (2006) in *Building Teams, Building People*, "Effective organizations . . . spread out the tasks, giving each person a 'piece of the action'" (p. 20). Strong leaders will seek to involve people at all levels of their educational system to support higher student achievement.

YOU HAVE TO ATTEND TO THE PERSONAL SIDE

When I reflect on the opportunity I had to serve as a superintendent for a school district in San Diego County, I first think of the people, not the accomplishments or trials. The single most important thing to me, then and now, is the relationships I was able to form with classified staff, teachers, administrators, parents, and board members during my tenure.

In fact, each year we would celebrate with a "Back to School Breakfast Celebration" prior to the first day of school. At that breakfast I had the opportunity to address 500–600 of our employees. We would take a lot of pictures during the school year of staff and children and put together a video montage with theme music of "us" doing great things and having a good time. The whole purpose of this event was to build and instill the importance of relationship. My address was purposively focused on the power of relationship and the importance of believing in our collective ability to accomplish what we set out to do to support all children in our district.

If you think about your career and life experience, we believe you will also find that relationships are a key part of your past. Kouzes and Posner (2002) clearly understand and advocate the importance of relationships in organizations and small teams when they write:

> Success in leadership, success in business, and success in life has been, is now, and will continue to be a function of how well people work and play together. We're even more convinced of this today than we were twenty years ago. Success in leading will be wholly dependent upon the capacity to build and sustain those human relationships that enable people to get extraordinary things done on a regular basis (p. 21).

Building and sustaining relationship is not a skill set or personality that a leader needs to be blessed with at birth. There is a wealth of literature addressing strategies and activities one can learn and tap into to support their leadership role in building strong relationships among teams.

One area of focus that needs to be addressed in all teams is the existence of conflict. Teams are composed of people and when you bring a group of people together to work toward a common purpose, there will be conflict of perceptions and ideas (Lencioni, 2005). Conflict can arise from several sources within the team including unmet needs among team members, a team member's preference versus seeking the best solution or outcome, too high an expectation, and poor communication skills such as making it personal rather than sticking with the issue (Beebe, Beebe, and Redmond, 2002; Harvey and Drolet, 2006).

Managing conflict when it surfaces has a positive impact on the building of effective teams and contributes to the building of trust among the members (Wiseman, 2008). Schwartz (2002) makes this point when he wrote: "An effective group considers conflict a natural part of group life; if it is managed well, conflict improves members' ability to accomplish their task, work together, and contribute to personal growth" (p. 24).

If the purpose of collaborative teams is to work together to accomplish the extraordinary goal of higher student achievement, then one of the keys to their success will be to foster stronger relationships among the members. Harvey and Drolet (2006) emphasize the importance of building relationships among team members and suggest that it is strong relationships that will help team members feel more collegial and motivated to accomplish great things. LaFasto and Larson (2001) build a strong case for the importance of relationships on teams and point out that failure to build and sustain relationships is a reason why teams fail. To reach the goal of higher achievement for all students the evidence is clear that successful leaders should consciously focus on building positive relationships among team members and encourage others to do the same.

CELEBRATE HIGH ACHIEVEMENT

Early in my administrative career I worked in a district that believed celebrating achievement was something that happened with and for key administrators. They would tout the success of the district in terms of administrative contributions and rarely acted deliberately to celebrate the many successes of other individuals or team efforts regarding student achievement. Although they employed similar strategies to other districts that were positively impacting student achievement in a sustainable fashion, this district was not making significant gains and morale was tepid at best among teachers and middle manager administrators.

Some of you may have found yourself in this situation working for a district or school site that did not understand the importance of celebrating achievement in a way that recognizes those who are contributing to that achievement. I know for the teachers and myself at my site there were feelings of being devalued and open discussions about "why bother" or "they do not really appreciate what we do."

Fortunately my career path took me to another district that understood the power of celebrating the success of individuals and teams regarding important accomplishments toward student achievement. The key leadership of this district understood the research that supports the importance of celebrating individual contributions as a powerful tool for building and sustaining effective teams (Harvey and Drolet, 2006; DuFour et al., 2006).

You may be familiar with the saying "what gets celebrated, gets done." When it comes to student achievement and the importance of teams, we propose that systemic celebration of high student achievement at all levels will perpetuate success and motivate individuals on teams and within an organization.

Fortunately there is considerable research that supports our proposal and the importance of the team principle, "Celebrate high achievement." McLaughlin and Talbert (2006) in their book about strategies to improve student achievement support the importance of celebrating student achievement at all levels in an organization. Tom Peter (1987) points out the importance of celebrating performance and wrote, "Well-constructed recognition settings provide the single most important opportunity to parade and reinforce the specific kinds of new behaviors one hopes others will emulate" (p. 307).

DuFour reminds us about the importance of celebrating high achievement in *Learning by Doing* when stating, "Recognition provides opportunities to say, 'Let us all be reminded, let us all know again, what is important, what we value, and what we are committed to do. Now let's all pay tribute to someone in the organization who is living that commitment'" (DuFour et al., p. 28).

Celebrating successes will motivate and empower team members to strive to reach their purpose (Harvey and Drolet, 2006). If you are serious about raising student achievement, be vigilant and systemic about finding opportunities to celebrate small and large achievements toward raising student achievement.

Therefore, the following are five principles that will help to strengthen teams:

1. High-achievement environments cannot exist without high-functioning teams.
2. Everybody must row in the same direction.
3. Everybody has a role in high achievement.
4. You have to attend to the personal side.
5. Celebrate high achievement.

PRACTICAL SUGGESTIONS

1. Examine all teams to see that they have high expectations as a primary purpose.
2. Purposively provide resources such as time, money, all pertinent data, and professional development opportunities for teams that are doing the work of increasing student achievement.
3. Use the district newsletter/website to share and recognize the student achievement successes of teams/sites and so forth.
4. Throw a party—picnic or district barbecue—to celebrate student success. Personally invite the team members across the district. An added recognition would be to let them invite family members. Include some fun activities and speak to the whole group about the important vision for all students achieving and their contributions.

5. Take the time to write handwritten notes to all team members to praise and recognize their efforts and success. Do this regularly and thoughtfully to include the many contributors/teams.
6. Every day take a few moments to reflect on how you are doing with reinforcing the importance of relationships and managing conflict.
7. Establish norms for teams and revisit them on a regular schedule.
8. Encourage team members to think of possibilities for increased student achievement and to try new ideas.

SOME BOOKS, ARTICLES, AND WEBSITES TO SUPPORT THE STRENGTH OF TEAMS

Buenrostro, S. *Closing the academic achievement gap on the California high school exit exam (CAHSEE) through professional learning communities (PLC) characteristics.* 2012. Doctoral dissertation retrieved from http://library.laverne.edu/.

DuFour, R., and R. DuFour. *Professional learning communities at work: Bringing the big ideas to life.* Bloomington, IN: Solution Tree. 2011.

DuFour, R. P., and Others. *Learning by doing: A handbook for professional learning communities at work.* Bloomington, IN: Solution Tree. 2006.

Feger, S., and E. Arruda. *Professional learning communities: Key themes from the literature.* Providence, RI: The Education Alliance, Brown University. 2008.

Firestone, W. A., and M. C. Martinez. "Districts, teacher leaders, and distributed leadership: Changing instructional practice." *Leadership and Policy in Schools.* 2007: 6(1), pp. 3–35.

Grubb, W. N., and J. J. Flessa. "A job too big for one: Multiple principals and other nontraditional approaches to school leadership." *Educational Administration Quarterly.* 2006: 42(4): pp. 518–550.

Harris, A., & Lambert, L. *Building leadership capacity for school improvement.* Berkshire, UK: Open University Press. 2003.

Harvey, Thomas, and Bonita Drolet. *Building teams, building people: Expanding the fifth resource.* Lanham, MD: Scarecrow Education. 2006.

Hill, L., and K. Lineback. *HBR Blog Network.* Retrieved from the *Harvard Business Review* website: http://blogs.hbr.org/hill-lineback/2011/07/the-fundamental-purpose-of-you.html?utm_source=feedburner&utm_medium=feed&utm_campaign=Feed%3A+harvardbusiness+(HBR.org).

Hiller, N. J., D. V. Day, and R. J. Vance. "Collective enactment of leadership roles and team effectiveness: A field study." *Leadership Quarterly.* 2006: 17(4), pp. 387–397.

Hord, S. M. *Professional learning communities: Communities of continuous inquiry and improvement.* Austin, TX: Southwest Educational Development Laboratory. 1997.

Hord, S. M. *Professional learning communities: What are they and why are they important?* Austin, TX: Southwest Educational Development Laboratory. 1997.

Jackson P., and H. Delehanty. *Sacred hoops: Spiritual lessons of a hardwood warrior.* New York: Hyperion. 1995.

Katzenbach J. R. *Why pride matters more than money: The power of the world's greatest motivational force.* New York: Crown Business. 2003.

Katzenbach, J. R., and D. K. Smith. "The discipline of teams." *Harvard Business Review.* 1993: 4428, pp. 111–120.

Katzenbach, J. R., and D. K. Smith. *The wisdom of teams: Creating the high-performance organization.* New York: HarperCollins Publishers, Inc. 2003.

Kouzes, J., and Barry Posner. *Leadership: The challenge* (3rd ed.). New York: Jossey-Bass. 2002.

Kruse, S., K. S. Louis, and A. S. Bryk, *Building professional community in schools. Issues in Restructuring Schools.* Madison, WI: Wisconsin Center for Education Research. 1994. Retrieved August, 12, 2012, from http://www.learner.org/workshops/principals/materials/pdf/kruse.pdf.

La Fasto, F., and C. Larson. *When teams work best,* Thousand Oaks, CA: Sage Publications. 2001.

Leithwood, K., and B. Mascall. *Collective leadership effects on student achievement.* Educational Administration Quarterly. 2008: 44(4), 559–61.

Lencioni, P. *Overcoming the five dysfunctions of a team: A field guide.* San Francisco, CA: Jossey-Bass. 2005.

McLaughlin, M. W., and J. E. Talbert. *Building school-based teacher learning communities: Professional strategies to improve student achievement.* New York: Teachers College Press. 2006.

Mealiea, L., and R. Baltazar. "A strategic guide for building effective teams." *Public Personnel Management.* 2005: 34(2), pp. 141–160.

O'Reilly, C., and J. Pfeffer. *Hidden value: How great companies achieve extraordinary performance with ordinary people.* Boston, MA: Harvard Business School Press. 2000.

Peters, T. *Thriving on chaos: A handbook for a management revolution.* New York: Knopf. 1987.

Reichstetter, R. "Defining a professional learning community" (E&R Report No. 06.05). 2006. Retrieved August 14, 2012 from http://www.wcpss.net/evaluation research/reports/2006/0605plc_lit_review.pdf .

Schwartz, R. *The skilled facilitator: A comprehensive resource for consultants, facilitators, managers, trainers, and coaches.* San Francisco: Jossey-Bass. 2002.

Simon, M. L. *Principals' and teachers' perceptions in the degree of Hord's five dimensions of PLCs between high-achieving middle school professional learning communities and high-achieving non-PLC schools.* (University of La Verne). 2012. Retrieved from ProQuest Dissertations and Theses, 324: http://search.proquest.com/docview/963967801?accountid=25355. (963967801).

Ulrich, D. "Credibility x capability." 1996.

Wiseman, P. P. *Professional learning communities and the effectiveness of the teams within those communities.* (University of La Verne). 2008. Retrieved from ProQuest Dissertations and Theses, 282-n/a: http://search .proquest.com/docview/304 385850?accountid=25355. (304385850).

Wiseman, P. P. *Strong schools, strong leaders: What matters most in times of change.* Lanham, MD: Rowman & Littlefield Education. 2010.

Chapter Ten

Collaboration and Shared Decision Making

The decisions we make today will shape the future for all of us for decades to come.

—Alan Mulally, President & CEO, Ford Motors

The importance of decision making has been a focus of discussion and literature for years—from the early work of prophets and seers with interpretations of dreams, to the meaning of tea leaf patterns, through the modern body of literature discussing many different theoretical decision-making models or frameworks. Most of the focus has been on decision- or problem-solving steps/models. This can be important, but if we want to really focus on decisions that will impact student achievement, it is important to focus on the people involved with the decisions.

It is one thing to study data and make an informed decision in isolation. It is a whole different approach to involve in the process the people who may be impacted by a decision and successfully implementing that decision.

I am reminded of my first principal position and the smoking lounge decision. Yes, this was back in the day of smoking lounges. Prior to my arrival at the school the majority of staff had been complaining about the few that smoked in the staff lounge. The previous principal made a unilateral decision that the staff lounge would be the "official" designated smoking area and those who were put off by smoking could eat in the large office/teacher workroom. When I arrived this issue had become volatile. The workroom was cluttered, busy, and smelled of duplicator chemicals. The only faculty restrooms were in the staff lounge so nonsmokers had to go to the smoking area to use the restrooms. Nonsmoker teachers were openly hostile to the smokers for taking over their staff lounge and in the past they had been friends. Given the emotion and destructiveness to relationships of this issue I decided to take it on the first few weeks of my arrival. I implemented a decision team of smokers, nonsmokers, the office manager, and the custodian to review all the possible solutions to determine if we could find a win-win solution. After a couple of meetings we were able to identify a small storage room off the book room that could be ventilated and used for a smoking area. Since there were only four smokers on staff they agreed to make the change for the good of all faculty. Within three weeks of taking on the problem in a collaborative process, we had diffused a very volatile situation. Within the first month after the change, teacher relationships were significantly improving. Fortunately, by the end of the year, smoking on campus was eliminated by California law.

The art of decision making that focuses on the "people" who will successfully implement those activities/strategies that lead to higher student achievement and high-achieving schools can be found in the following six principles.

THE WHAT GOES DOWN, BUT THE HOW GOES UP

The concept of "the what goes down and the how goes up" is a key factor for increasing student achievement. The board and superintendent should have a vision for change that is focused on actions and strategies to support increased student achievement. However, the accomplishment of that vision will depend on the leadership's ability to involve teachers, classified staff, and parents in the determination of the actions necessary to make the vision a reality.

The "what goes down" is not a new concept (Witt, Andrews, and Kacmar, 2006) and the top down legislative-mandated change has become woven into the fabric of educational legislation with No Child Left Behind and Race To The Top being prime examples of the "what comes down." I had the pleasure to serve as superintendent for a number of years in a successfully achieving school district and do not recall Congress having a personal chat with me about the many facets of the NCLB law in regards to what the legislature decided needed to happen to improve student achievement. However, they are not shy about legislating the "what."

We can all identify with statements like, "They do not have a clue about the real world in the classroom," or "There is no way our students can meet those levels of achievement." These are just two examples of many you could come up with that illustrate the frustration among administrators, teachers, and staff that leads to an outcome of self-doubt and lack of believability. We don't believe that there is anything they can do to bring about positive change given the top down, mandated, legislative requirements; continuing lack of resources; and the inability to control many socioeconomic factors that can influence student achievement.

Another reality, however, is that in your leadership role to provide vision and direction it may be necessary for you to provide the "what" when it comes to changes needed to focus on improving student achievement.

I can recall many times as superintendent when I was the person determining the "what" down within my district. One time in particular was the decision to develop a standards-based report card for grades kindergarten through sixth grade to help us focus on improving student achievement and communicating our efforts with children and parents.

That caused uproar with our upper-grade teachers and the teacher representatives of the local bargaining unit that resulted in what started as a confrontational meeting with me, a union-led representation of teachers, and my assistant superintendent of education. It was necessary for me to explain the "why" of the decision and be clear that this was the direction we as a district would be taking based on our district vision and board/superintendent direction. However, I was quick to explain that the "how" we develop and get to a working standards-based report card was open to their full participation.

I made it clear we would work and make decisions on the "how" together and if it took a year, or even two years ,we would have a standards-based report card that was collaboratively developed. This hardworking team, led by my assistant superintendent, did produce an exemplary standards-based report card that was adapted for use in other districts and was used by the IDMS System developed by the Pullium Group.

Yes, it is true that stakeholders across a school district may not have much say about the "what" that goes down. However they should have a loud voice in the "how." As educational leaders, superintendents need to move our teachers, staff, parents, and community beyond the negative and resistant reaction of others telling us what we must do, to helping them understand that they are empowered and encouraged to fully participate in the "how" regarding the decision process and implementation of mandated change.

Like the standards-based report card story, if we want to empower stakeholders to focus on change that results in greater student achievement, they need to understand and believe that determining how to implement positive change is a very important role for making decisions that will positively impact student achievement.

As a K–12 consultant, I have visited some sites and districts where the climate is one of doom and gloom. When talking with them I often hear statements like, "We are doing the best we can with the little we have," or "Our budget has been cut so badly there is really no way we can meet the needs of all our students." These are clear indicators that these folks are focused on what they cannot do rather than what they might be able to accomplish, even in tough economic times.

Beware of becoming bogged down in the centrifuge of negative reactions to mandated change. Become the leader that empowers teachers, staff, and parents to make meaningful decisions on how to implement meaningful change to support student achievement.

There have been a number of popular experts that emphasize the importance of planned learning community (PLC) practices such as Senge (2006), Hord (1997), and DuFour (2011). Recent studies by Arroyo (2011), Simon (2012), and Buenrostro (2012) focused on the PLC practices of Hord (1997) and DuFour (2011) and the impact of these practices on student achievement.

These studies looked at high-achieving schools and all three studies found a strong link between leadership that sought the involvement and input of teachers, parents, and students, and student achievement. Focusing on "the what goes down and the how goes up" will support student achievement within the district and at individual school sites.

SHARING THE INFORMATION LEADS TO ACHIEVEMENT-BASED DECISIONS

You are probably familiar with the saying "What you don't know won't hurt you." Well this may be the case when someone is trying to not worry about something they cannot control. However I have certainly found that what I did not know has hurt me in the realm of life and decision making.

I vividly remember the speeding ticket I received for doing 76 in a 65 zone that was monitored by camera enforcement. The law in that state was you could not be ticketed by photo enforcement unless you were traveling at 10 plus miles over the speed limit. I dutifully set my cruise control at 73 mph and thought all was good. When I received the ticket in the mail with my smiling face behind the windshield of my car, I was certainly not pleased. What I found I did not know was that the custom tires on my new care negatively impacted the accuracy of my speedometer so what I thought was 73 mph was actually 76. In that case I was hurt by the tune of $185 for what I did not know!

You may have had a similar personal or professional decision-making experience when you thought you were making the correct decision and, in fact, found out it was not, given information that was not known by you at the time. It is these experiences that cause us to see new meaning to another saying: "It's what you don't know that can hurt you" (Nutt, 2002). In other words, decision making by its very nature is about dealing with uncertainty. It is uncertainty that can make many decisions, difficult; and difficult decisions, very difficult.

Now I do not propose that we can become totally omniscient as decision makers. Sometimes decisions are made on how we feel or what Buchanan and O'Connell (2006) call making decisions by the "romance of the gut." We are always going to have a level of uncertainty regarding our rational decision making whether it is from a lack of information or actions based on our emotions (Simon 1991).

However, we can and should seek to find out about what we don't know and then strive to share all that we do know with those involved with making a decision that impacts student learning. It takes time and effort to equally inform all decision-making participants, research the data and discuss what they do not know, but this can yield strong decisions that will lead to real change for increasing student achievement.

If we want to empower our stakeholders to make the best decisions for enhancing student achievement, then they need to be given access to all information that can impact the outcome of their decision. As a golfer I appreciate the importance of knowing the distance to the green, the slope of the green, the hazards that may surround the green, and the wind factor so I can select the appropriate club so I can place the ball close to the cup with my approach shot.

The same is true for decision making that leads to increased student achievement. The decision makers need as much information available (student data, current research, current practices, etc.) so they can make the appropriate decisions that will allow students to reach their highest achievement potential.

WHERE THERE IS PARTICIPATION THERE IS INVESTMENT; WITH INVESTMENT COMES SUCCESS

The importance of shared or participative decision making has been acknowledged and touted for many years as a key to increasing student achievement at the site and district level. Unfortunately the way many leaders implemented shared decision making is best illustrated by a comment I heard from a middle school teacher while consulting for the district. When I asked about how shared decision making worked for teachers, she responded "Oh great, they make all the decisions and then share them with us."

It was clear the "they" was in reference to administration at the site and district level and that she did not feel as though she was a participant in the decision-making process.

Now this is cute little saying that has been around for some time, but it is grounded in the reality that too many of our leaders do not, as evidenced by their actions, embrace the importance of empowering teachers, parents, along with administrators to be part of the "how comes up" decision making. This has been a problem for years as evidenced by a variety of states legislating shared decision making, such as HB 940 passed by the Kentucky legislature that mandated participation of teachers and parents in decision making that impacted policy and student achievement.

The importance of greater participation in decision making has a vast history of supportive research studies over the years. When teachers, staff members, and parents are left out of the decision-making process they often feel disconnected and little or no ownership to support change that is directed at improving student achievement.

The opposite of this "Why bother, no one asked us!" takes place when a leader embraces greater participation in the important decision-making" at the site and the district. Witt, Andrews and Kacmar (2000) conducted a study about the role of participation in decision making and concluded that participation "can reduce uncertainty, increase understanding of events, and, as shared information is to some extent shared power, lead to feeling of control" (p. 351). In other words, participation can result in greater understanding of the issues, and a feeling of empowerment as one of the decision makers and can lead to less resistance to implementation.

Increasing participation does result in a positive investment toward student achievement. Remember the Kentucky bill passed in 1990? Today, twenty-two years later, the website for the Kentucky Department of Education states "making decisions through shared decision making results in a greater commitment to implementing decisions that will enhance the achievement of students."

Kentucky School districts and the state's Department of Education cite the power of HB 940 for producing positive change at all levels of the K–12 system in Kentucky from curriculum to finance. They cite the School Based Decision Making (SBDM) Model established and empowered by HB940 as leading to decisions critical to increasing student achievement by allowing local districts and sites to participate in budget, staffing and curriculum decisions that best fit their student population needs. One of the key components of this SBDM approach is the inclusion and participation of administrators, teachers, classified staff, and parents in the decision-making process.

The importance of increased participation for school site decision making is well established. The Kentucky experience has tied that increased stakeholder participation to the making of decisions that has resulted in increased student achievement. It is important to note that the Kentucky Department of

Education, to this day, provides tremendous support to all districts in the form of professional development and specialized training for the SBDM process. They also publish a quarterly newsletter to provide support and information regarding SBDM.

THE BROADER THE INVOLVEMENT THE BETTER

The previous principle is focused on the concept that actively involving the people of your district in the important decision making efforts will produce clear definitions of the actual problem, the number of solutions and the likelihood of selecting the best option for that particular issue. This principle is focused on the "who" of the decision-making process. Who will be included needs to be crafted thoughtfully and who will be making the decision needs to be clear to all participating in the process. (Harvey and Broyles, 2011)

School districts are composed of administrators, teachers, staff, parents, bargaining units and community members that represent diverse positions, thoughts and perceptions regarding decisions that focus on improving student achievement. Thoughtful involvement of constituents across this spectrum of diverse perceptions and agendas is critical to the quality and resulting implementation of decisions made by a participatory process. This broad involvement of constituents does lead to better decisions that focus on student achievement for all students.

A caveat to remember is that having a seat at the table does not mean having the power to make the decision. It means being invited to the conversation. I remember a mentor of mine reminding me that "important people have a say, but that does not mean they will get their way."

In regards to the "who" will be involved, I recall years ago in my district establishing a special education advisory board that was a delight to work with in the beginning. The participants were cobbled together to represent stakeholders across the district; however, they were mostly folks of like mind and agreement who were perceived to be supportive.

As time progressed ,what seemed like good, well-thought-out decisions were again and again met with tremendous resistance from those most impacted. This resistance surfaced in forms of nonimplementation, parent protest regarding program changes involving their special needs child, and at times, grievances filed by certificated and classified bargaining units. We thought we were involving people in the decision-making process but it soon became clear it was not the "right" group of people. The next year the advisory board was thoughtfully restored to include a more diverse representation.

People who had demonstrated an ability to work collaboratively with others were purposively selected to represent a broader spectrum of opinions and different agendas. This change in the "who" was involved on the advisory board resulted in a more positive outcome regarding decisions made and success of implementation/acceptance. It did require more time to discuss alternatives to determine the "how" we wanted to make a change to increase the achievement of our special needs children. However, once the decision was made, the support for implementation was widespread and there was far less resistance.

For instance, the second year that the thoughtfully selected advisory board was in place it recommended a complete change in how we deliver services to special needs children that would result in moving many of them back to their actual home school of residence versus the one they were being bused to each day. We were making the right decision for our children's needs, but I admit to having been nervous about the pending public school board meeting scheduled to present the requested change. Although there were some folks who did speak about their concerns for the change proposed, most supported implementing the change.

The most significant thing for me was that when people did speak about being apprehensive about the change, they would usually include a statement to the effect of, "I am not really supportive of this change because I am concerned how it will impact my child, but I do understand why it is being proposed."

The inclusion of parents across this spectrum of diverse perceptions and agendas on the advisory board resulted in a broad base of understanding the "why"s for this change. The plan was implemented with very few problems the next school year and it is still in place.

A second critical part to actualizing this principle is the thought given and clarity of understanding about the "who" will be making the decision. We have all had an experience of being part of a team that had an understanding or perception that we would be making a decision as part of our work, and then hearing the words from those in positional power: "We appreciate your input and take it under advisement." Later a decision is made that reflects little or none of what the team had recommended.

This type of leadership leads to a lack of trust for the decision-making process and stakeholders in the district will not want to participate in the future, making statements like, "Why bother? They will do what they want no matter what we think."

There is a place for directive decision making as well as collaborative or participatory decision making. If my grandson is about to step off the curb into moving traffic I am not about to seek collaboration with his parents before making a decision and taking action! The problem that can exist in organizational leadership is to view every decision as collaborative or as a directive decision such as my grandson example. They both have advantages and a place in decision making, but a more productive approach is to be thoughtful and combine both directive and collaborative decision making.

Harvey's (2001) Directive Collaboration Decision-Making Model provides a guide for blending both approaches. Harvey (2001) states that combining these two approaches will allow the leader to select the best of both and "increases his chance of effective, long-term change" (p. 139).

Lastly, there is the importance of stakeholder involvement and the "buy-in" from participants that is important for successful implementation of change that impacts student achievement.

In the past decade there have been volumes published on the importance of the Professional Learning Community (PLC) approach to school decision making and the positive impact on student achievement (Arroyo, 2011; Du-Four and DuFour, 2011; Hord, 1997). Although there is still need for more research to provide a clear link between PLCs and student achievement, the evidence for participation in decision making and implementation has been established. In a recent study published by Arroyo (2011) he concluded, "To promote collective learning and application among the PLC's members, the first strategy was recognizing the importance of and seeking the buy in of all PLC members when making application decisions. A second strategy was the administrator was to trust the collective will of the PLC and go with their desired applications."

GOOD DECISION PROCESS SAVES TIME

Time is a valuable resource and one that we constantly seek more of in the K–12 system. We all have likely had a less-than-positive experience working with a team to make a decision about some change to improve student achievement. Further, decisions made that do not incorporate the principles cited in this chapter often take longer to structure and can result in a time-consuming implementation process that yields less-than-favorable results or misses the intended outcome completely. This type of scattered decision making can rob a district of time and cause the superintendent and other key leaders to spend far more time in answering questions, explaining the "why," and defending the process/decision.

Many scholars in the past have written about the leader and the leader's role in decision making. Much of what was written in the past emphasized the role of a single leader making decisions for the organization. Today the role of the leader is more about leading the decision-making process than making the decision individually and then asking others to implement that decision. Vroom and Jago (1974) understood the nature of decision making by a leader as more of a "social process with the elements of the process presented in terms of events between people rather than events that occur with a person" (p. 743).

Given the social nature of decision making, it is important to implement the principles of this chapter. Doing so will seem to be unnecessary to the person that just wants to "do it," but good process during the decision-making process can save considerable time of a leader and those involved in the decision-making process.

The research supports at least two ways good decision making can lead to a saving in time. Productivity is one of those outcomes from good decision making that can save time. When stakeholders are part of the decision making there is a great increase in commitment that results in an increase in productivity, thus utilizing the resource of time to its fullest. A second outcome is improved morale. When stakeholders feel valued in the decision-making process the gap of discontent is narrowed and less time is spent on defending, and more time spent on raising, student achievement.

We often hear from educational leaders that there is just not enough time. A good decision-making process that leads to strong buy-in for implementation can save up to 30 percent of the time spent on the alternative of making decisions for all and then hoping they will "see the light" and implement. That savings of time is time that can be refocused on improving student achievement rather than explaining and defending "why" you are making a change or implementing a new curriculum.

GOOD DECISION-MAKING WITHOUT IMPLEMENTATION DOES NOT YIELD CHANGE FOR SUCCESS

Once a change decision is made, the next, and perhaps the most critical, step is implementation. If we fail at implementing the decision across the district or school, then the impact intended for student achievement will be lost and possibly even set back. The need for implementing and sustaining change in public education has been an ongoing issue.

Girvin's (2004) study on implementing change supports this notion given her statement: "Since the change process is complex and the school environment constantly chaotic, schools are faced with many challenges to overcome if a change initiative is to survive" (p. 30).

Several change experts have addressed this need to plan for successful change implementation and most of them make it clear that the steps taken prior to implementing the change are as important as the those strategies used to support implementation. Kotter (1996) and Harvey (2001) both stress the need to begin the implementation process prior to the actual implementation.

Superintendents using the above principles will support a successful implementation by creating the power of the vision for all stakeholders and then communicating that vision, creating short-term wins, providing clarity and simplicity to reduce resistance, and selling the need for change throughout the decision-making process and implementation.

Therefore, the following six principles lead to collaboration and shared decision making:

1. The what goes down, but the how goes up.
2. Sharing the information leads to achievement-based decisions.
3. Where there is participation there is investment; with investment comes success.
4. The broader the involvement the better.
5. Good decision process saves time.
6. Good decision making without implementation does not yield change for success.

PRACTICAL SUGGESTIONS

1. Adopt a decision-making and problem-solving model that supports implementation.
2. *Use the Practical Decision Maker* (Harvey et al. 1997) Six-Step Approach is an action-oriented model that incorporates the common elements of several theoretical models. The six steps are: Mind-set; Problem Definition; Solution Criteria; Possible Solutions; Solution Choice; Implementation.
3. Consider the use of structuring devices for narrowing a choice once possible solutions have been generated in the group process. Some suggested structuring devices from *The Practical Decision Maker* (1997) are:
   - Multi-Voting
   - Priority Matrix
   - Payoff Matrix
   - Spend-a-Dot
4. Make sure all decisions have a "how" component, not just the "what."
5. Make clear to folks involved in decision making the type of decision they are discussing. The following four types of decisions from Jones and

Bearley (1994) provide a mental map for your understanding of the decision type:
- Consultation—group discusses and makes recommendations; the leader makes the decision. Involves information gathering/sharing prior to decision.
- Command—leader makes decision. Process is quick but should be used sparingly.
- Consensus—working with group to get them to move toward an agreement without serious disagreement from the parties involved. Supports implementation but not always possible for highly charged situations.
- Convenience—person or group makes decision by whatever manner is easiest. Good for small, somewhat unimportant decisions.

Use the following checklist when selecting the 'who' will be involved in a decision- making action or determining the how a decision impacting student achievement will be implemented. The list present possible participants, your role is to determine who "needs" to be involved in the process.

_____   Board member(s)

_____   Superintendent

_____   Cabinet member(s)

_____   Other District level representatives

_____   Site Principal(s)

_____   Teacher Bargaining Unit representative(s)

_____   Teachers impacted by decision and/or implementation

_____   Classified Bargaining Unit representative(s)

_____   Classified employee representatives impacted by decision and/or implementation

_____   Parent(s)

_____   Community representative(s)

_____   Student(s)

Chart 10.1.   Participation/Involvement Checklist

SOME BOOKS, ARTICLES, AND WEBSITES TO SUPPORT DECISION MAKING

Arroyo, Hector. *Strategies used by successful professional learning communities to maintain Hord's dimensions of PLCs and include new members.* (University of La Verne). 2011. Retrieved from ProQuest Dissertations and Theses: http://search.proquest.com/docview/896956740?accountid=25355.

Buchanan, L., and A. O'Connell. "Decision making." *Harvard Business Review.* January 2006: pp. 1–8.

Buenrostro, S. *Closing the academic achievement gap on the California high school exit exam (CAHSEE) through professional learning communities (PLC) characteristics.* 2012. Doctoral dissertation retrieved from http://library.laverne.edu/.

DuFour, R., and R. DuFour. *Professional learning communities at work: Bringing the big ideas to life.* Bloomington, IN: Solution Tree. 2011.

Girvin, N. *The use of nine factors for institutionalizing change to sustain a character education initiative in middle schools.* (University of La Verne). 2004. Retrieved from ProQuest Dissertations and Theses: http://search.proquest.com/docview/305103322?accountid=25355.

Harvey, T. R. *Checklist for change: A pragmatic approach to creating and controlling change.* Lanham, MD: Scarecrow Press, Inc. 2001.

Harvey, T. R., W. L. Bearley, and S. M. Corkrum. *The practical decision maker: A handbook for decision making and problem solving in organizations.* Lancaster, PA: Technomic Publishing Company, Inc. 1997.

Harvey, T., and E. Broyles. *Resistance to change: A guide to harnessing its positive power.* Lanham, MD: Rowman & Littlefield Publishers, Inc. 2010.

Hord, S. M. *Professional learning communities: Communities of continuous inquiry and improvement.* Austin, TX: Southwest Educational Development Laboratory. 1997.

Hord, S. M. *Professional learning communities: What are they and why are they important?* Austin, TX: Southwest Educational Development Laboratory. 1997.

Jones, J. E., and W. L. Bearley. *Teambook.* King Of Prussia, PA: HRDQ. 1994.

Kotter, J. P. *Leading change.* Boston, MA: Harvard Business School Press. 1996.

Nutt, P. C. *Why decisions fail.* San Francisco: Berrett-Koehler Publishing, Inc. 2002.

Senge, P. M. *The fifth discipline: The art and practice of the learning organization* (Rev. ed.). New York: Doubleday. 2006.

Simon, M. L. *Principals' and teachers' perceptions in the degree of Hord's five dimensions of PLCs between high-achieving middle school professional learning communities and high-achieving non-PLC schools.* (University of La Verne). 2012. Retrieved from ProQuest Dissertations and Theses, 324: http://search.proquest.com/docview/963967801?accountid=25355. (963967801).

Vroom, V. H., and A. G. Jago. "Decision making as a social process: Normative and descriptive models of leader behavior." *Decision Sciences.* 1974: 5, pp. 743–769. doi: 10.1111/j.1540-5915.1974.tb00651.x.

Witt, L. A., M. C. Andrews, and K. M. Kacmar. "The role of participation in decision making in the organizational politics-job satisfaction relationship." *Human Relations.* 2000: 53, pp. 341–358.

Chapter Eleven

Communication

The message you send is the message you receive.

—Harvey and Drolet

It is a truism of any organization that communication is a must for that organization to function well. But, if it is so true, then why do we do it so poorly? From looking at hundreds of institutions, we find that communication problems are the most common and persistent ones in those organizations. It is easy to conceptualize the solutions to these problems, but hard to do.

We worked with an international communications company that was involved in making communication devices for the U.S. Army. They didn't believe in having secretaries or phone answerers. When we got there, their biggest problem was, you guessed it, communications. Executives spent so much time answering their own phones that they didn't have time for meetings or collaboration. We tried to do something about it but they weren't interested in hearing us. We were there to do "something else." They went out of business two years later. The problem was obvious but they weren't listening. Will you?

As for high-achieving environments, it is necessary to communicate and communicate and communicate about achievement.

These are the principles about that communication:

USE ALL AVENUES AND DO THEM OFTEN

Whether it may be in writing or given orally or e-mail or in the form of newsletters or given in a staff meeting or told to a parent, you must emphasize all avenues of communication and that communication must emphasize the importance to you and your district of high achievement. You can't say it enough.

One organization we worked with had a satellite campus in trailers. Computers were nonexistent. Messages went out to everyone in the district routinely by e-mail. The satellite campus knew nothing, attended nothing and was isolated from communications. One day the superintendent thought to call and ask why there was not representation at meetings, why reports weren't completed, and so on. He was surprised to hear nothing had been received by them. You see, all communications were by one means—e-mail.

You must diversify your messages. You use all avenues. You also must be persistent in your communication. You must, as politicians say, stay on "message." You have to celebrate all kinds of achievement—athletic, academic, artistic, vocational, whatever. Staying on message means:

1. Figuring out what you want to say about achievement,
2. Crafting the message,
3. Saying in all avenues of communication your messages,
4. Repeating your message.

Your expectations for high achievement never go unsaid. You must say them over and over and over again (Munter, 2011).

COMMUNICATE THAT HIGH ACHIEVEMENT IS FOR ALL

Emphasis on achievement isn't just the province of one group of constituents. You should expect achievement from all regardless of ethnicity or age or ability or whatever. Ongoing achievement may be different for GATE students versus developmentally delayed students. But each can achieve in his/her own way.

You can expect women to do as well as men in math or shop. You can expect blacks and Hispanics to do as well as their Caucasian counterparts in academics. You can expect men to do as well as women in art. You can expect older adults to do as well as younger adults in your continuing education programs. You can expect students, teachers, parents, classified staff, and administrators to emphasize and share excellence in what they individually and collectively do. No, achievement is not just for one group.

As mentioned in chapter 4, expectations are everything. In a classic study of expectations known as the Pygmalion Effect (Rosenthal and Jacobson, 1992), they found that expectations of achievement can lead to significant achievement gains. This study has been repeated over the years. Cooper and

Good (1983) hold that "once an expectation is held, an individual tends to act in ways that are consistent with the belief and eventually his or her actions may cause the expectations to become a reality." What you expect to achieve is a self-fulfilling prophecy.

With the Pygmalion Effect in mind, you need to communicate to all that you expect high achievement from all.

USE TWO-WAY COMMUNICATION

Feedback is important to get high achievement. There is much evidence on the necessity of feedback for student learning (sourcesofinsight.com, NWEA, 2013). It is equally true that it is necessary for management (performance-appraisals.org). At its heart, feedback is simply two people talking together, in whatever form, and giving information about the performance of each other. It is two-way communication (Munter, 2011; Perkin, 2010; Barker and Gaut, 2002). Necessary for two-way communication are:

1. A sender of information, and
2. A receiver of that information that is able and willing to hear it,
3. A receiver of information that is willing to send back messages to the sender. (Munter, 2011)

Too often, though, we practice one-way communication. We talk at our audience, without hearing from them. Equally problematic is that we never check to see if the receiver got the message. And even worse, we never give the receiver a chance to give back information.

If we practice one-way communication and we never check for receipt of our talking, we practice bad teaching techniques and bad management. We don't encourage engagement and investment. Without these latter two, our schools become depositories of rote learning and sabotage.

It takes more effort and patience to use two-way communication, but without it, you are doomed to an effortless, low-achieving environment. Feedback provides the means of personal development and change. Without it, you're stuck where you are.

To achieve a high-achieving environment you need to:

1. Walk around a lot using informed channels of communication (you can't just stay in your office).
2. Ask questions of everyone.
3. Ask for feedback.

4. Communicate with joy (morose environments do not equal high-achieving environments).
5. Communicate often.
6. Listen a lot.

THE MESSAGE YOU SEND IS THE MESSAGE YOU RECEIVE

We have long used the euphemism, "The message you send is the message you will receive." If you stay in your office and do one-way communication, you will receive messages back like, "I don't care," "Let me alone," "When is school over?" and best of all, "do I have to?" If on the other hand, you walk around, ask a lot of questions, act joyful, and talk about achievement of all sorts, then you will get back lots of talk about achieving and a joyful, high-achieving environment.

I have an acquaintance who never ventures out from his office and never hugs or laughs or cries. Students see him as uncaring and aloof. He wonders why. He cares but he doesn't show it.

On the other hand, my wife is always asking kids questions and hugging them. They love her. And she loves them back.

Did you ever see adults talking to babies? They coo and make faces and smile. They do this not only to communicate with the child, but also to express their love and to be loved back.

The message you send is the message you receive. If you want high achievement and joy, you need to express high achievement and joy.

The following four principles lead to good communication:

1. Use all avenues and do them often.
2. Communicate that high achievement is for all.
3. Use two-way communication.
4. The message you send is the message you receive.

PRACTICAL SUGGESTIONS

These are some practical suggestions to implement communication:

1. Write weekly newsletters—What better way to get the word out about achievement than a weekly newsletter. They should emphasize achievement in all forms—academic, athletic, artistic, vocational, and so forth.

You can tell stories. You can announce awards about achievement. You can restate your goals and vision. The newsletter can be printed on paper or Web-based.

By emphasizing achievement you can say to all that this is a high-achieving environment.

2. Emphasize achievement at meetings—At your teacher or administrative meetings have a standing item on your agenda "Progress toward Achievement." You can talk about what progress you have made toward helping students achieve and what you can do to make them achieve even more. You can talk about your goal of having a high-achieving environment. You can keep your staff's "eye on the prize."

Even better, have teachers share success stories in small groups and then illustrate one or two of them on a chart. They can be hung in the library or lobby.

3. Form a service club—Whether it is in Rotary or Lions or Kiwanis or Soroptimists or Chamber of Commerce, you can constantly tell the story of your school/district's commitment to achievement. You must communicate with the public and give them the positive message that your schools are there to succeed. You must overcome the negative news about ineffective schools and how they are "falling short." You must couple this with positive stories. Remember you need the local communities. They elect school board members and vote on bond issues. Don't just go to them when you need them. Tell the positive stories constantly. Ask your service club to honor a teacher or student each month for their exceptional work. One school had a committee whose charge it was to drop in on exceptionally high-achieving classrooms with a plaque and flowers.

There are many ways to show recognition for a job well done. Try one.

4. Practice MBWA—The abbreviation stands for "Management By Walking Around." You can't stay in your office and hope to convey your message. You must go to the teachers'/administrators' lounge or visit people in their office or see students at recess. You need to ask them the following questions:
   - What did you excel in this week?
   - Did you see someone else succeed this week? Tell me the story.
   - What are you proud of?
   - How can you do better?
   - How can the school help you to achieve?

Now once you have answers, don't just let them be forgotten. Do something with the responses and make sure people notice. Walk the talk.

5. Remember the #1 Goal—If you haven't done so already, have one or more goals on achievement. Build it into your vision. Most importantly, build it

into your strategic plan and your action plans. Have clear and measurable steps to achieving your goals of attaining a high-achieving environment. The goals then need to be evaluated consistently. Are we moving toward them? How do we know? What data do we have? Do we need to do more?

6. Give out pins—As hokey as it seems, people love pins. Give out each week or month pins to employees and students who have achieved this month. Invite parents to come to board meetings to see their sons/daughters pinned. At assemblies, announce the names of winners and why they got them. I was a city councilman and at the beginning of each meeting, we would recognize citizens for something. In fact, we were dubbed the city of "pins, plaques, and proclamations." Our citizens loved them. They valued them. They sought to repeat what they did to earn them. And incidentally, we were reelected time and time again. If you recognize people for achievement, you'll get achievement.

SOME BOOKS, ARTICLES AND WEBSITES TO SUPPORT COMMUNICATION

Barker, Larry, and Deborah Gaut. *Communication* (8th ed.) Boston, MA: Allyn & Bacon. 2002.

Barrett, Deborah. *Leadership communication.* New York: McGraw-Hill. 2009.

Becker, Ethan, and Jon Wortmann. *Mastering communication at work: How to lead, manage and influence.* Englewood Cliffs, NJ: Prentice Hall. 2009.

Condrill, Jo, and Bennie Bough. *101 ways to improve your communication skills instantly* (5th ed.). Englewood Cliffs, NJ: Prentice Hall. 2012.

Griffin, E. M. *A first look at communication theory.* New York: McGraw-Hill. 2009.

Hackman, Michael, and Craig Johnson. *Leadership: A communication perspective.* Long Grove, IL: Waveland Press. 2009.

Knapp, Mark, and Judith Hall. *Nonverbal communication in human interaction.* Holt, Rhinehart. 1992.

Munter, Mary. *Guide to managerial communication.* Englewood Cliffs, NJ: Prentice Hall. 2011.

Perkins, P. S., and Les Brown. *The art and science of communication.* Hoboken, NJ: John Wiley & Sons.

Rosenberg, Marshal. *Non-violent communication.* Encinitas, CA: PuddleDancer Press. 2003.

Rosenthal, R., and L. Jacobson. *Pygmalion in the classroom.* (Expanded ed.). New York: Irvington. 1992.

Chapter Twelve

Flexibility and Resilience

Educators must anticipate change and head the parade to avoid becoming victims of change.

—Thomas R. Harvey

I had a colleague who was the guru of change. He demanded innovation and fostered technological change. The trouble was he was hopelessly intolerant and inflexible. Every time you dared to disagree with him, he flew off the handle and ranted and raved. He didn't demonstrate that which he professed.

The attitude of flexibility and resilience is a very important stepping stone to a high-achieving environment. In this world of endless change, you must be flexible enough to adapt and resilient enough to get up from your failures.

BE RESILIENT

Part of success is failure. You can't know success unless you know failure.

Resilience is getting knocked down and getting back up. It is simple as that. Now, it doesn't feel good to experience failure. It can be depressing and demoralizing. But it cannot lead to immobilization. Inaction is the enemy of resilience.

There are four qualities that make up resilience:

1. Problem-Solving Skills.
   This involves critical thinking and discernment. Do you have the ability to define the problem? Can you come up with a workable solution? Will you

implement the chosen solution? If you can do all these things, you have problem-solving skills.

2. Sense of Personal Control.

Do you have a feeling that your destiny is in your own hands? The psychologists call it "internal focus of control," which is a fancy way of saying what you do will affect what happens to you. You have a sense of personal potency.

3. Support from Friends.

Not only should your friends give personal support, but they should also give critical but loving feedback on what you are doing. Both are important.

4. Action.

Do something. Act. Serve others. The only way to get over your depression with your personal failing is to set out a program of action and then do it. If you don't know what to do, then merely serve others until some problem-solving skills kick in. Inaction is the enemy of psychological health (Neenan, 2009).

The last quality is most important—you have got to keep doing something to create a high-achieving environment. Success is worth it.

And in being resilient, you model resiliency and flexibility for others. You must not hide your feelings. This just makes you seem invulnerable. Air them. Share them. Seek input on them. You'll find sharing your failures with others will only lead to later success.

ADAPTATION AND PERSISTENCE

In biology the organism that survives is the one that adapts. In schools, if you don't adapt, if you rigidly stick to what you are doing, you will soon become outmoded and passé.

In the 21st Century School movement, adaptability is one of the seven key skills that all students and their leaders must have (Wagner, 2008; Harvey, 2011). In this world of change, you must be prepared to alter what you are doing and seek out something better.

You must be prepared to adapt the ideas and suggestions in this book, as well as all ideas, to meet your circumstances. If not, you'll not achieve a high success environment.

But at the same time you are adapting, you must be persistent in what you do. You must give the change a chance to work. If you abandon an idea the first time you experience some resistance, you'll never be successful. Change requires time and persistence to implement it.

I remember in the eighties I wanted to put a greater emphasis on teacher teaming. The teacher was resistant. I was persistent. I knew what was needed. I persisted in the "what" of change.

But teachers had to have a hand in developing teams. They had to determine the "how" of change (chapter 10). So I constituted an ad hoc committee to design how teacher teams would work. Eventually, they implemented it and it was hugely successful.

Now, it may not seem like a big deal today, but then it was. But by being both persistent and flexible I achieved my end.

The best way to deal with this apparent paradox is to remember persistence equals "what" and flexibility equals "how." You must be persistent in setting out the overall picture of what you hope to achieve. You must set goals and be reasonably persistent with them. But when it comes to how we are going to achieve them or the objective we are going to shoot for, you must be flexible and adaptive. Obviously you should abandon goals that no longer work. But give them a long, hard look before you abandon them.

FROM ADVERSITY COMES STEEL

While in college, I worked at Bethlehem Steel. I saw raw iron ore put in a big cauldron and then put under intense heat. The slag was thrown off and all that was left was the molten steel.

So, too, is it with human lives. We apply intense heat and pressure to our raw beings and some just give in to the pressure and give up. They become human slag. But most are simply made stronger by the pressure and become better for it. Sure the fire is no fun and we hate every minute of it. But it makes us stronger. From adversity comes steel.

I remember seeing Joe Plom give a speech. He started by walking three paces to the left. He then turned around and walked three paces to the right. He repeated this motion several times. Then he spoke. He had been a Vietnam POW and that was all the room he had in his "tiger cage." He was there for two years. He could have gone mad. But instead he did three things each day:

1. He played in his mind every shot of some golf course he played.
2. He talked to his God.
3. He thought of advice he'd give his children when he eventually returned.

He kept strong in the face of captivity by overcoming the pain of confinement and torture and thinking instead about what he would do. From adversity comes steel.

I remember Anne Breitenberger. She was dying from cancer. The faculty all met and expressed that while she was our best doctoral graduate that year, she couldn't get out of her bed and be the doctoral banner carrier. But we decided we'd ask her out of courtesy to her record.

When we did, we were amazed. She said yes. When graduation came, she got out of her bed and dressed in her regalia. She came to the stadium and carried the doctoral banner. With someone on each side of her, she went step by step by step by step down the center aisle. When later asked about her feat, she said, "I wouldn't miss this for the world. I earned it. I enjoyed it." Three weeks later she died. But she was an inspiration to us all. From adversity comes steel.

Finally, I remember vividly having a debilitating stroke. The doctors all said I would never walk or talk again. They wanted to warehouse me in a nursing home. I was feeling sorry for myself. But my wife came to the hospital. She looked me square in the eye and said, "You always speak about from adversity comes steel. Now prove it." That challenge was all that I needed. It was hard, painful work to learn how to walk again. It was frustrating to have to relearn speech. It was incredibly demoralizing having to learn to smile again. It took me about a year in the hospital in-patient and out-patient wards. But I did it. And I'm better off for it. From adversity comes steel.

Now, how does this relate to establishing a high-achieving environment? You'll get knocked down in your quest. You'll fail. But you have got to get up and brush yourself off and learn from your mistakes. If you say to yourself, "From adversity comes steel," then you'll have the fortitude to achieve success.

Therefore, the following three principles lead to flexibility and resilience:

1. Be Resilient.
2. Adaptation and persistence.
3. From adversity comes steel.

PRACTICAL SUGGESTIONS

These are some practical suggestions to implement flexibility and resilience.

1. Print buttons.
   • Print up and wear a button that says, "Success is Worth It."
   • Print up and wear a button that says, "From Adversity Comes Steel."
2. Say a mantra.
   • Say five times a day, "Success is worth it."
   • Say five times a day, "From adversity comes steel."
3. Fill out:

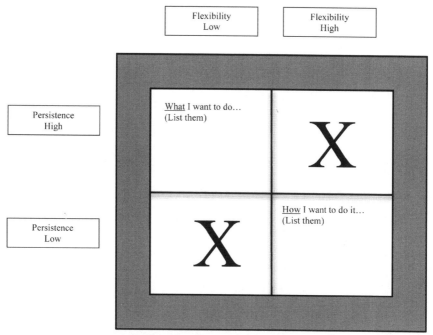

Chart 12.1. Persistence and Flexibility Chart

SOME READINGS WORTH NOTING

Gurvis, Joan, and Allan Calarco. *Adaptability: responding effectively to change.* Pfeiffer Center for Creative Leadership. 2007.

Harvey, Thomas. *21st century schools.* La Verne, CA: EPIC Monograph. 2011.

Neenan, Michael. *Developing resilience.* New York: Routledge. 2009.

Reivich, Karen, and Andrew Shatte. *The resilience factor.* New York: Broadway Books. 2002.

Ryan, M.J. *Adaptability: how to survive change you didn't ask for.* New York: Broadway Books. 2009.

Wagner, Tony. *The global achievement gap.* New York: Random House. 2008.

Chapter Thirteen

A Concluding Note

These then are the stepping stones to crafting a high-achieving environment. They are easy to talk about but hard to do. You are highly skilled in some of these and not in others.

On the following pages is a scale for each principle you must achieve. The degree to which you are on the right side of the scale is the degree to which you have mastered the action. Conversely, the degree to which you are on the left side of the scale is the degree to which you have to work on this to craft a high-achieving environment.

It is not inputs that matter—how "good" the students are, how much money you have, or how up-to-date the facilities are. These all help but they are not the major determinants. It is what you do. The processes that you pursue and the actions you take determine whether or not you have a high-achieving environment.

Fill out the scales. Check them out for accuracy of perception with four to five teachers. Talk over your results with other district administrators or principals. But you must attend to these principles if you want to craft a high-achieving environment.

High Achievement Environment Scale

(HAES)

Do I:	Not At All		Somewhat		To a Great Degree	
Establish a Clear Vision for the Organization	1	2	3	4	5	N/A
Develop and Adhere to Goals that Focus on Student Achievement	1	2	3	4	5	N/A
Encourage the Good Ideas of Others	1	2	3	4	5	N/A
Do the Right Thing (Versus Doing Things Right)	1	2	3	4	5	N/A
Use Collaboration	1	2	3	4	5	N/A
Manage the Relationships of the Institution	1	2	3	4	5	N/A
Turn a Toxic Environment Around	1	2	3	4	5	N/A
Establish Trust	1	2	3	4	5	N/A
Make People Want to be There	1	2	3	4	5	N/A

Do I:	Not At All		Somewhat		To a Great Degree	
Use Norms	1	2	3	4	5	N/A
Use Artifacts, Heroes and Stories	1	2	3	4	5	N/A
Know My Staff Members' Stories and Honor Them	1	2	3	4	5	N/A
Celebrate	1	2	3	4	5	N/A
Use Joy	1	2	3	4	5	N/A
Have High Achievement as a Goal	1	2	3	4	5	N/A
Have Values	1	2	3	4	5	N/A

Do I:

	Not At All		Somewhat		To a Great Degree	N/A
Do Strategic Planning	1	2	3	4	5	N/A
Have All Constituents Buy-in to the Vision	1	2	3	4	5	N/A
Have Low Expectations for Students	1	2	3	4	5	N/A
Have High Expectations for Students	1	2	3	4	5	N/A
Give support for High Expectations	1	2	3	4	5	N/A
Love the People I Work With	1	2	3	4	5	N/A
Love the Work	1	2	3	4	5	N/A
Practice Skills of Love	1	2	3	4	5	N/A
Act as a Good Finder	1	2	3	4	5	N/A

Do I:	Not At All	Somewhat	To a Great Degree		N/A
Make Student Learning the Chief Responsibility of Everyone	1	2	3	4	5	N/A
Set High Expectations for Learning	1	2	3	4	5	N/A
Define Rigor	1	2	3	4	5	N/A
Demand Rigor	1	2	3	4	5	N/A
Support Rigor	1	2	3	4	5	N/A
Establish Technology as a Focus of Professional Development Priorities and Goals	1	2	3	4	5	N/A

Do I:	Not At All	Somewhat	To a Great Degree	
See Professional Development as an Intensive, Ongoing and Connected Practice	1	2	3	4	5	N/A
Align Professional Development with School Improvement Priorities and Goals	1	2	3	4	5	N/A
Use School Based Coaching to Enhance Professional Learning	1	2	3	4	5	N/A
Establish Mentoring and Induction Programs for New Teachers	1	2	3	4	5	N/A
Use Teacher Self-assessed Needs, Evaluation Needs, and Student Achievement needs to propel Professional Development	1	2	3	4	5	N/A
Use Assessments for 21st Century Skills	1	2	3	4	5	N/A
Employ Formative Assessment	1	2	3	4	5	N/A

Do I:

	Not At All		Somewhat		To a Great Degree	
Use Multiple Assessments	1	2	3	4	5	N/A
Use Data Over and Over Again	1	2	3	4	5	N/A
Use Data Assiduously to Improve	1	2	3	4	5	N/A
Use Trend Data	1	2	3	4	5	N/A
Use as Team to Analyze Data	1	2	3	4	5	N/A
Change Assessments for Common Core Standards	1	2	3	4	5	N/A
Use Criteria that are Authentic	1	2	3	4	5	N/A

Do I:

	Not At All	Somewhat		To a Great Degree		
Make Sure I Have a High Functioning Team	1	2	3	4	5	N/A
Make Sure that Everybody Goes in the Same Direction	1	2	3	4	5	N/A
Make Sure I Have a Role in High Achievement	1	2	3	4	5	N/A
Attend to the Personal Side of Teams	1	2	3	4	5	N/A
Make Sure the What Goes Down, But the How Goes Up	1	2	3	4	5	N/A
Share the Information	1	2	3	4	5	N/A
Use Participation to Get Investment Success	1	2	3	4	5	N/A
Broaden the Involvement	1	2	3	4	5	N/A

Do I:	Not At All	Somewhat	To a Great Degree		N/A
Implement Good Decision Making Practices	1	2	3	4	5	N/A
Use All Avenues of Communication	1	2	3	4	5	N/A
Communicate that High Achievement Is for All	1	2	3	4	5	N/A
Use Two-way Communication	1	2	3	4	5	N/A
Behave Resiliently	1	2	3	4	5	N/A
Practice Adaptability	1	2	3	4	5	N/A
Practice Persistence	1	2	3	4	5	N/A
Have a High Achieving Environment	1	2	3	4	5	N/A

References

"Academic rigor." Olympic Educational Services District #114 in Bremerton, WA. (www.oesd.wednet.edu).

Adams, John. *Miracles at work.* New London, CT: Life Without Limits Press. 2005.

Arroyo, Hector. *Strategies used by successful professional learning communities to maintain Hord's dimensions of PLCs and include new members.* (University of La Verne). 2011. Retrieved from ProQuest Dissertations and Theses: http://search.proquest.com/docview/896956740?accountid=25355.

Barker, Larry, and Deborah Gaut. *Communication* (8th ed.). Boston, MA: Allyn & Bacon. 2002.

Barnes, F. D. *Making school improvement part of daily practice.* Annenberg Institute for School Reform at Brown University. 2004. Retrieved on August 12, 2012 from Annenberg Institute website: http://annenberginstitute.org/tools/guide/SIGuide_intro.pdf.

Barrett, Deborah. *Leadership communication.* New York: McGraw-Hill. 2009.

Becker, Ethan, and Jon Wortmann. *Mastering communication at work: How to lead, manage and influence.* Englewood Cliffs, NJ: Prentice Hall. 2009.

Beebe, S., and M. Redmond. *Interpersonal communication: Relating to others.* Boston, MA: Allyn & Bacon. 2002.

Bennis, W. G. *On becoming a leader.* Cambridge, MA: Perseus Publication. 2003.

Bennis, Warren, and Burt Nanus. *Leaders: Strategies for taking charge.* New York: Harper & Row. 2003.

Berlew, D. E., and D. T. Hall. "The socialization of managers: Effects of expectations on performance." *Administrative Science Quarterly*, September 1966: 208.

Bilanech, Bud. *Using values to turn a vision into reality.* Amazon. 2000.

Black, P., C. Harrison, C. Lee, B. Marshall, and D. Wiliam. "Working inside the black box: Assessment for learning in the classroom." *Phi Delta Kappan.* 2004: 86(1), 9–21.

Black, P., and D. Wiliam. "Inside the black box, raising standards through classroom assessment." *Phi Delta Kappan.* October 1998: 80, 139–148.

135

Black, P., and D. Wiliam. "Developing the theory of formative assessment." *Educational Assessment, Evaluation, and Accountability*. 2009: 21(1), 5–31. doi: 10.1007/s11092-008-9068-5.

Blair, Tony. Daily Mail Online.com on Sunday, 1994.

Broullitte, Liane. *Charter schools: Lessons in school reform in topics in educational leadership.* Lawrence Erlbaum Assocs. 2009.

Bryson, John. *Strategic planning for public and non profit organizations*. San Francisco: Jossey Bass. 1995.

Buchanan, L., and A. O'Connell. "Decision making." *Harvard Business Review*. January 2006: 1–8.

Buenrostro, S. *Closing the academic achievement gap on the California high school exit exam (CAHSEE) through professional learning communities (PLC) character-istics*. 2012. Doctoral dissertation retrieved from http://library.laverne.edu/.

Carnegie, Andrew. BrainyQuote.com. Retrieved December 31, 2012 from BrainyQuote.com website: http://www.brainyquote.com/citation/quotes/quotes/a/andrewcarn130735.htm#6v0iswkkUCBcOgzt.00.

Carnegie, Andrew. *Winston Churchill leadership*. Retrieved on July 28, 2012 from Winston Churchill Leadership website: http://www.winston-churchill-leadership.com/leadership-quote-part2.html.

Cartwright, Taluka, and David Baldwin. *Communicating your vision*. Greensboro, NC: Center for Creative Leadership. 2006.

Cashman, Kevin. *The pause principle*. San Francisco: Berrett-Koehler. 2012.

Chappuis, Jan, Rick J. Stiggins, Steve Chappuis, and Judith A. Arter. *Classroom assessment for student learning: Doing it right—Using it well* (2nd ed.). Pearson. 2011.

"A college readiness issue brief: Academic rigor: At the heart of college access and success." Washington, DC: Pathways to College Network. 2009.

Collins, James. *Good to great*. New York: HarperCollins. 2001.

"Common core state standards and assessments." Created and posted on Oklahoma State Department of Education (OSDE) Common Core State Standards (CCSS) website. May 20, 2001. Retrieved from http://ok.gov/sde/sites/ok.gov.sde/files/C3May20ppt.pdf.

Condrill, Jo, and Bennie Bough. *101 ways to improve your communication skills instantly* (5th ed.). NJ: Prentice Hall. 2012.

Cordingley, Philippa, and Others. *The impact of collaborative Continuing Professional Development (CPD) on classroom teaching and learning*. 2005. http://wsas-sets.s3.amazonaws.com/ws/nso/pdf/09598003e49523abff794962e2752c81.pdf.

Corporate Leadership Council. *Driving performance and retention through employee engagement*. Washington, DC: Corporate Executive Board. 2004.

Covey, S. R. *The seven habits of highly effective people: Powerful lessons in personal change*. New York: Simon and Schuster. 2004.

Curtis, Mark, and Thomas Harvey. *Project Athena: An evaluation of the grants programs of the National Endowment of Humanities*. Washington, DC. 1976.

Daggett, Willard R. *Achieving academic excellence through rigor and relevance*. International Center for Leadership in Education. 2012.

Daggett, W. R. *Effectiveness and efficiency framework—A guide to focusing resources to increase student performance.* Retrieved on August 29, 2012 from International Center for Leadership in Education website: http://www.leadered.com/pdf/EE%20%20White%20Paper%20website%203.25.09.pdf.

Darling-Hammond, Linda, and Frank Adamson. *Beyond basic skill: The role of performance assessment in achieving 21st century standards of learning.* Stanford Center for Opportunity Policy in Education (SCOPE), Stanford University, School of Education. Retrieved from http://edpolicy.stanford.edu.

Darling-Hammond, L., and M. W. McLaughlin. "Policies that support professional development in an era of reform." *Phi Delta Kappan*, 1995: 76(8), 597–604.

Darling-Hammond, Linda, Ruth Chung Wei, Alethea Andree, Nikole Richardson, and Stelios Orphanos. *Profession learning in the learning profession: A status report on teacher development in the united states and abroad.* Stanford, CA: National Staff Development Council, Stanford University. 2009.

Deal, Terrence, and Peterson, Kent. *Shaping school culture.* San Francisco: Jossey-Bass. 2009.

Delpit, L. *Other people's children: Cultural conflict in the classroom.* New York: The New Press. 1995.

Drolet, Bonita and Deborah Turner. *Building a bridge to success: From program improvement to excellence.* Lanham, MD: Rowman & Littlefield. 2010.

DuFour, R. "Leading edge: 'Collaboration lite' puts student achievement on a starvation diet." *Journal of Staff Development.* 2003: 24(3), 63–64.

DuFour, Rick. "Why celebrate? It sends a vivid message about what is valued." *Journal of Staff Development*, Fall 1998: 19(4).

DuFour, R., and R. DuFour. *Professional learning communities at work: Bringing the big ideas to life.* Bloomington, IN: Solution Tree. 2011.

DuFour, R. P., and Others. *Learning by doing: A handbook for professional learning communities at work.* Bloomington, IN: Solution Tree. 2006.

Edmonds, R. "Effective schools for the urban poor." *Educational Leadership.* 1979: 37(1), 15–27.

Education Connection's Center for 21st Century Skills, 355 Goshen Road, PO Box 909, Litchfield, CT 06759, 860.567.0863, Fax: 860.567.3381. Retrieved from http://www.skills21.org/.

Farr, S. *Teaching as leadership: The highly effective teacher's guide to closing the achievement gap.* San Francisco; Jossey-Bass. 2010.

Fay, Jim, and David Funk. *Teaching with love and logic.* Golden, CO: Love and Logic Press. 1995.

Feger, S., and E. Arruda. *Professional learning communities: Key themes from the literature.* Providence, RI: The Education Alliance, Brown University. 2008.

Firestone, W. A., and M. C. Martinez. "Districts, teacher leaders, and distributed leadership: Changing instructional practice." *Leadership and Policy in Schools.* 2007: 6(1), 3–35.

Fletcher, Jerry. *Patterns of high performance.* San Francisco: Berrett-Koehler Publishers. 1993.

Formative Assessments, STEM. Retrieved from http://www.stemresources.com/index.php?option=com_content&view=article&id=52&Itemid=70.

Ghaye, Tony. *Teaching and learning through reflective practice: A practical guide for positive action.* Taylor & Francis. 2011.

Gilman, Cheryl, *Doing the work you love.* Chicago: Contemporary Books. 1997.

Girvin, N. *The use of nine factors for institutionalizing change to sustain a character education initiative in middle schools.* (University of La Verne). 2004. Retrieved from ProQuest Dissertations and Theses: http://search.proquest.com/docview/305 103322?accountid=25355.

Goddard, Goddard, and Tschannen-Moran. "A theoretical and empirical investigation of teacher collaboration for school improvement and student achievement in public elementary schools." *Teachers College Record.* 2007: 109(4), 877–896.

Goldsmith, H. F., and R. Beckhard. (Eds.). *The leader of the future: new visions, strategies, and practices for the next era.* San Francisco: Jossey-Bass. 209–219.

Green, R. L. *Expectations: How teacher expectations can increase student achievement and assist in closing the achievement gap.* Columbus, OH: McGraw-Hill. 2005.

Griffin, E. M. *A first look at communication theory.* New York: McGraw-Hill. 2009.

Grubb, W. N., and J. J. Flessa. "A job too big for one: Multiple principals and other nontraditional approaches to school leadership." *Educational Administration Quarterly.* 2006: 42(4): 518–550.

Gurvis, Joan, and Allan Calarco. *Adaptability: Responding effectively to change.* Pfeiffer Center for Creative Leadership. 2007.

Hackman, Michael, and Craig Johnson. *Leadership: A communication perspective.* Long Grove, IL: Waveland Press. 2009.

Harris, A., & Lambert, L. *Building leadership capacity for school improvement.* Berkshire, UK: Open University Press. 2003.

Harvey, Thomas. *21st century schools.* La Verne, CA: EPIC Monograph. 2011.

Harvey, T. R. *Checklist for change: A pragmatic approach to creating and controlling change.* Lanham, MD: Scarecrow Press, Inc. 2001.

Harvey, T. R., W. L. Bearley, and S. M. Corkrum. *The practical decision maker: A handbook for decision making and problem solving in organizations.* Lancaster, PA: Technomic Publishing Company, Inc. 1997.

Harvey, T. R., and E. A. Broyles, *Resistance to change.* Lanham, MD: Rowman & Littlefield Publishers. 2010.

Harvey, Thomas, and Bonita Drolet. *Building teams, building people: Expanding the fifth resource.* Lanham, MD: Rowman & Littlefield. 2006.

Haycock, K. "Closing the achievement gap for native students." *The Huffington Post.* July 12, 2012. Retrieved September 19, 2012 from http://www.huffingtonpost.com/kati-haycock/achievement-gap-native-students_b_1672247.html.

Haycock, Kati, "Education Trust leader Kati Haycock addresses Lesley Leadership Council." October 19, 2012. Retrieved from http://news.lesley.edu/2012/10/education-trust-leader-kati-haycock-addresses-lesley-leadership-council.shtml.

Hill, L., and K. Lineback. *HBR Blog Network.* Retrieved from the *Harvard Business Review* website: http://blogs.hbr.org/hill-lineback/2011/07/the-fundamental-purpose-of-you.html?utm_source=feedburner&utm_medium=feed&utm_campaig n=Feed%3A+harvardbusiness+(HBR.org).

Hiller, N. J., D. V. Day, and R. J. Vance. "Collective enactment of leadership roles and team effectiveness: A field study." *Leadership Quarterly.* 2006: 17(4), 387–397.

Hord, S. M. *Professional learning communities: Communities of continuous inquiry and improvement.* Austin, TX: Southwest Educational Development Laboratory. 1997.

Hord, S. M. *Professional learning communities: What are they and why are they important?* Austin, TX: Southwest Educational Development Laboratory. 1997.

Jackson P., and H. Delehanty. *Sacred hoops: Spiritual lessons of a hardwood warrior.* New York: Hyperion. 1995.

Jacoby, J. "The role of educational leadership in ensuring academic success for every child." *New Horizons for Learning.* 2003. Retrieved from the Johns Hopkins University website: http://education.jhu.edu/PD/newhorizons/Transforming%20Education/Leadership%20in%20Education/The%20Role%20of%20Educational%20 Leadership%20in%20Ensuring%20Academic%20Success%20for%20Every%20 Child/index.html.

Jerald, Craig. *School culture: The hidden curriculum.* Reading Rockets. December 2006. Retrieved from http://www.readingrockets.org/article/26095/.

Jobs, Steve. Stanford commencement address by Steve Jobs. *Stanford UMV News, Stanford Report.* June 14, 2005.

Jones, J. E., and W. L. Bearley. *Teambook.* King of Prussia, PA: HRDQ. 1994.

Katzenbach J. R. *Why pride matters more than money: The power of the world's greatest motivational force.* New York: Crown Business. 2003.

Katzenbach, J. R., and D. K. Smith. "The discipline of teams." *Harvard Business Review.* 1993: 4428, 111–120.

Katzenbach, J. R., and D. K. Smith, *The wisdom of teams: Creating the high-performance organization.* New York: HarperCollins Publishers, Inc. 2003.

"Key to business success: Love the work you do." 2011. Retrieved from Getoutfromunderyourbusiness.com.

Knapp, Mark, and Judith Hall. *Nonverbal communication in human interaction.* Holt, Rhinehart. 1992.

Kotter, J. P. *Leading change.* Boston, MA: Harvard Business School Press. 1996.

Kouzes, J., and Barry Posner. *Leadership: The challenge* (3rd ed.). New York: Jossey-Bass. 2002.

Kouzes, James, and Barry Posner, *Encouraging the heart.* San Francisco: Jossey-Bass. 2003.

Kouzes, J., and Barry Posner. *The leadership challenge* (4th ed.). San Francisco: Jossey-Bass. 2007.

Kruse, S. D., and K. S. Louis. *Building strong school cultures: A guide to leading change.* Thousand Oaks, CA: Corwin Press. 2009.

Kruse, S., K. S. Louis, and A. S. Bryk, *Building professional community in schools. Issues in restructuring schools.* Madison, WI: Wisconsin Center for Education Research. 1994. Retrieved August, 12, 2012, from http://www.learner.org/workshops/ principals/materials/pdf/kruse.pdf.

La Fasto, F., and C. Larson. *When teams work best.* Thousand Oaks, CA: Sage Publications. 2001.

Leithwood, K., and B. Mascall, "Collective leadership effects on student achievement." *Educational Administration Quarterly.* 2008: 44, 529–561.

Lencioni, P. *The five dysfunctions of a team.* San Francisco: Jossey-Bass. 2002.

Lencioni, P. *Overcoming the five dysfunctions of a team: A field guide.* San Francisco: Jossey-Bass. 2005.

Livingston, J. S. "Pygmalion in management (HRB classic)." *Harvard Business Review*, January, 2003: 5–12.

Louis, K. S., K. Leithwood, K. L. Wahlstrom, and S. E. Anderson. "Investigating the links to improved student learning: Final report of research findings." The Wallace Foundation. 2010. Retrieved from the Wallace Foundation website: http://www.wallacefoundation.org/knowledge-center/school-leadership/key-research/Pages/Investigating-the-Links-to-Improved-Student-Learning.aspx.

March, James. "Understanding how decisions happen in organizations." In Zue Shaprira (Ed.), *Organizational decision making.* New York: Cambridge University Press. 1997: 9–34.

Marzano, R. J. "High expectations for all." *Educational Leadership.* September 2010: 68(1), 82–84. Retrieved from http://www.ascd.org/publications/educational-leadership/sept10/vol68/num01/High-Expectations-for-All.aspx.

May, Daniel. "Building the cultural artifacts of the organization." *The Maersk Institute*, University of Southern Denmark, Odense, Campusvej 55, Odense M DK-5230, Denmark, dmay@mip.sdu.dk.

McLaughlin, M.W., and J. E. Talbert. "Contexts that matter for teaching and learning." Stanford, CA: Center for Research on the Context of Secondary School Teaching, Stanford University. 1993.

McLaughlin, M. W., and J. E. Talbert. *Building school-based teacher learning communities: Professional strategies to improve student achievement.* New York: Teachers College Press. 2006.

Meador, Derrick. "Common Core Assessment: An overview of the Common Core Standards Assessment." 2012. Retrieved from http://teaching.about.com/od/assess/a/Common-Core-Assessment.htm.

Mealiea, L., and R. Baltazar. "A strategic guide for building effective teams." *Public Personnel Management.* 2005: 34(2), 141–160.

Muller, Robert D., "Defining rigor in high school: Framework and assessment tool." Washington, DC: National High School Alliance. 2006.

Munter, Mary. *Guide to managerial communication.* Prentice Hall. 2011.

Nanus, Burt. *Visionary leadership.* San Francisco: Jossey-Bass. 1992.

Neenan, Michael. *Developing resilience.* New York: Routledge. 2009.

Nevills, Pamela, *Build the brain for reading: Grades 4–12.* Corwin Press. 2011.

Newmann, F., and G. Wehlage. *Successful school restructuring.* Madison, WI: Center on Organization and Restructuring of Schools. 1995.

Nutt, P. C. *Why decisions fail.* San Francisco: Berrett-Koehler Publishing, Inc. 2002.

O'Reilly, C., and J. Pfeffer. *Hidden value: How great companies achieve extraordinary performance with ordinary people.* Boston, MA: Harvard Business School Press. 2000.

P21 toolkit; A guide to aligning the Common Core State Standards with the Framework for 21st Century Skills. Retrieved from http://www.p21.org/storage/documents/P21CommonCoreToolkit.pdf.

Perkins, P. S., and Les Brown. *The art and science of communication.* Hoboken, NJ: John Wiley & Sons.

Peters, T. *Thriving on chaos: A handbook for a management revolution.* New York: Knopf. 1987.

Peterson, Kent D., a professor in the Department of Educational Administration at the University of Wisconsin-Madison. (http://www.educationworld.com/a_admin/admin/admin275.shtml) (coauthor of *Shaping School Culture: The Heart of Leadership*).

Peterson, Kent D., NCREL Monograph: *Building collaborative cultures: seeking ways to reshape urban schools.* 1994. Retrieved from http://www.ncrel.org/sdrs/areas/issues/educatrs/leadrshp/le0pet.htmi#author.

Phillips, G. *Classroom rituals for at risk learners.* Vancouver, BC: EduServ, British Columbia School Trustees Publishing. 1996.

Pielstick, Dean. "Beyond vision: The transforming leader." 2006. Retrieved from www.cha.nav.edu/pielstick 2006.

ProfessionalLearningcommunities.http://books.google.com/books?hl=en&lr=&id=J-TETSs7P6EC&oi=fnd&pg=PA1&dq=embedded+professional+development+education&ots=Q96rIqqBRZ&sig=WARmXshVnvSVKv4eXFX1a087N4#v=onepage&q=embedded%20professional%20development%20education&f=false.

Rath, T., and B. Conchie. *Strengths based leadership: Great leaders, teams, and why people follow.* New York: Gallup Press. 2008.

Reflective Practice http://books.google.com/books?hl=en&lr=&id=cBP-oO0bTesC&oi=fnd&pg=PP1&dq=embedded+professional+development+education&ots=5DKhdwNWjp&sig=zvVRFcLUuobQrYxhtwWCAYio64M#v=onepage&q&f=false.

Reichstetter, R. "Defining a professional learning community" (E&R Report No. 06.05). 2006. Retrieved August 14, 2012 from http://www.wcpss.net/evaluation research/reports/2006/0605plc_lit_review.pdf .

Reivich, Karen, and Andrew Shatte. *The resilience factor.* New York: Broadway Books. 2002.

Rosenberg, Marshall, "Non-violent communication." Encinitas, CA: PuddleDancer Press. 2003.

Rosenthal, R., and L. Jacobson. *Pygmalion in the classroom* (Expanded ed.). New York: Irvington. 1992.

Roueche, Suanne D. (Ed.). *Innovation abstracts.* August 30, 2002: 24 (16).

Ryan, M. J. *Adaptability: How to survive change you didn't ask for.* New York: Broadway Books. 2009.

Savitz-Romer, Mandy, Jole Jager-Hyman, and Ann Coles. "Executive summary: Removing roadblocks to rigor: Linking academic and social supports to ensure college readiness and success." Washington, DC: Pathways to College Network. April 2009.

Schwartz, R. *The skilled facilitator: A comprehensive resource for consultants, facilitators, managers, trainers, and coaches.* San Francisco: Jossey-Bass. 2002.

Senge, P. M. *The fifth discipline: The art and practice of the learning organization* (rev. ed.). New York: Doubleday. 2006.

Shaw, George Bernard. *Pygmalion*. New York: Brentano. 1916.

Simon, Herbert. "Bounded rationality and organizational learning." *Organization Science*. 1991: 2 (1), 125–134. doi:10.1287/orsc.2.1.125.

Simon, M. L. *Principals' and teachers' perceptions in the degree of Hord's five dimensions of PLCs between high-achieving middle school professional learning communities and high-achieving non-PLC schools*. (University of La Verne). 2012. Retrieved from ProQuest Dissertations and Theses, 324: http://search.proquest.com/docview/963967801?accountid=25355. (963967801).

Southwest Educational Development Laboratory. "Vision, leadership and change." *Issues . . . about Change*. 2(3).

Stiggins, R., J. Arter, J. Chappius, and S. Chappius. *Classroom assessment for student learning: Doing it right, using it well*. Assessment Training Institute. 2006.

Strong, Michael. *Mentoring new teachers to increase retention: A look at the research*. Santa Cruz: New Teacher Center, University of California Santa Cruz. 2005.

"Taking center stage—Act II." California Department of Education (CDE). 2011. Retrieved August, 2012, from http://www.cde.ca.gov/ci/gs/mg/cefmgtcsii.asp.

The Hechinger Institute. *Understanding and reporting on academic rigor: A Hechinger Institute primer for journalists*. New York: Teachers College, Columbia University.

Toms, Michael, and Justine Toms. *True work*. New York: Crown Publishing. 1998.

Tracy, Brian. *Maximum achievement*. New York: BPS Books. 2010.

Trontz, Randi. "Recognizing rigor in the classroom." 2013.

Tschannen-Moran, Megan. "Moran's scale." Retrieved from http://mxtsch.people.wm.edu/research_tools.php.

Tschannen-Moran, M., and Hoy Woolfolk. "A Teacher efficacy: Capturing an elusive construct." *Teaching and Teacher Education*. 2001: 17, 783–805.

Ulrich, D. "Credibility x capability." 1996.

Vroom, V. H., and A. G. Jago. "Decision making as a social process: Normative and descriptive models of leader behavior." *Decision Sciences*. 1974: 5, 743–769. doi: 10.1111/j.1540-5915.1974.tb00651.x.

Wagner, Tony. "Expecting excellence." *Rigor Redefined*. October 2008: 66(2), 20–25.

Wagner, Tony. *The global achievement gap*. New York: Random House. 2008.

Wagner and Masden-Copas. "School culture audit." Center for Improving School Culture. 2002.

Weiss, Alan. *Good enough isn't enough*. Amacom Book. 2000.

West Ed's healthy kids school climate survey. Retrieved from http://www.wested.org/chks/pdf/scs_flyer_04.pdf.

Wheatley, M. J. "Bringing schools back to life: Schools as living systems." Excerpted from *Creating successful school systems: Voices from the university, the field, and the community*. Christopher-Gordon Publishers. September 1999. Retrieved September 14, 2012, from http://www.margaretwheatley.com/articles/lifetoschools.html.

Wilson, Brady. *Love challenges all*. 2010.

Wiseman, P. P. *Professional learning communities and the effectiveness of the teams within those communities.* (University of La Verne). 2008. Retrieved from ProQuest Dissertations and Theses, 282-n/a: http://search .proquest.com/docview/304 385850?accountid=25355. (304385850).

Wiseman, P. P. *Strong schools, strong leaders: What matters most in times of change.* Lanham, MD: Rowman & Littlefield Education. 2010.

Witt, L. A., M. C. Andrews, and K. M. Kacmar. "The role of participation in decision making in the organizational politics-job satisfaction relationship." *Human Relations.* 2000: 53, 341–358.

Wylie, Caroline. "Part II: Formative and diagnostic assessment approaches in math & science." TeachersSERVCenter, University of North Carolina at Greensboro. March 22, 2010. Retrieved from http://www.serve.org/assessment-webinar.aspx.

Yoon, K. S., and Others. "Reviewing the evidence on how teacher professional development affects student achievement." *Issues & Answers Report.* REL 2007: No. 03. Washington D.C. U.S. Department of Education, Institute of Education Sciences, National Center for Education Evaluation and Regional Assistance, Regional Education Laboratory Southwest. Retrieved from http://ies.ed.gov/ncee/edlabs/regions/southwest/pdf/REL_2007033pdf and http://64.78.6.92/library/schoolbasedlitreview.pdf.

Ziglar, Z. *See you at the top* (2nd ed.). Gretna, LA: Pelican Publishing Company, Inc. 2000.

Index

About the Authors

Thomas R. Harvey is the Michael Abraham's endowed chair in Excellence in Leadership. He received his B.A. from Princeton University and his Ph.D. from Syracuse University. He has been teaching since 1970 in the departments of Organizational Leadership at Syracuse University, Claremont Graduate School, and the University of La Verne. He first came to La Verne as the director of Research, Evaluation, and Quality Assurance. He then became the Associate Dean of Graduate Education and then the Dean of the School of Organizational Management. In 2000  he went back to full-time teaching. He has taught such courses as Conflict, Change Theory, Team Building, Decision Making, Statistics, Research Methods, Leadership, Planning, and Organizational Theory and Evaluation, all to doctoral students. In 1990 he received the Excellence in Teaching Award; in 2004 he received the Ellsworth Johnson Faculty Service Award; and in 2006 he was named as an inaugural member of the Research Academy. He is the only member of the university to receive all three honors. He was a member of the La Verne City Council from 1984–2005. He has published ten books and innumerable articles.

Dr. Douglas P. DeVore is a tenured professor of Organizational Leadership for the University of La Verne Doctoral Program, where he is also Assistant Director of the Educational Policy Institute of California (EPIC). He received an Ed.D. from the University of La Verne. Prior to teaching at the University, Dr. DeVore was the superintendent of the Encinitas Union School District in California and was twice named K–12 Superintendent of the  Year by the North Costal Chapter of the Association of California School Administrators. He has served as the cochair of the Superintendents Technology and Advisory Committee for San Diego COE, President of the Association of Low Wealth School Districts in California, and serves as Assistant Director of the Educational Policy Institute of California (EPIC).

Dr. DeVore's academic efforts include refereed writing, presentations, and serving as a reviewer. He has published a number of peer-reviewed articles in the educational field and K–12 policy papers. His research is primarily focused on K–12 organizations with an emphasis on systems theory and leading change. As a consultant, Dr. DeVore brings over 40 years of leadership experience to a variety of organizational clients he continues to serve.

Dr. Bonita (Bonnie) Drolet is the coauthor of the best seller, *Building Teams, Building People: Expanding the Fifth Resource* that she wrote with Dr. Thomas Harvey and *Building a Bridge to Success: From Program Improvement to Excellence,* with Dr. Deborah Turner. Dr. Drolet is sought after by many school districts, government, and private enterprises to assist them in building successful organizations. She received her Bachelor of Arts and Master of Arts from California State University, Los Angeles. She received her Doctorate in Educational Management from the University of La Verne.

Her teaching career included elementary and middle school. She moved into administration becoming a principal for fourteen years. Her tenure as a principal included opening a new school—Bryant Ranch—that became a California Distinguished School and a National Blue Ribbon School within five years of its opening under her leadership.

As Assistant Superintendent of Educational Services, she was the curriculum leader for her district, which received multiple state and federal recognitions for achieving schools, innovative programs, and arts programs.

She has been selected as a leader of her many professional organizations and bestowed many recognitions and awards. She loves mentoring and coaching principals and district level administrators as well as strengthening the skills of classroom teachers.